a stitch in time

HEIRLOOM KNITTING SKILLS

a stitch in time
HEIRLOOM KNITTING SKILLS

RITA TAYLOR

A Quantum Book

First edition for North America and the Philippines published in 2013 by
Barron's Educational Series, Inc.

All inquiries should be addressed to:
Barron's Educational Series, Inc.
250 Wireless Boulevard
Hauppauge, New York 11788
www.barronseduc.com

ISBN: 978-1-4380-0195-1

Library of Congress Control Number: 2012948358

This book is published and produced by
Quantum Books
6 Blundell Street
London N7 9BH

QUMSTHK

Publisher: Sarah Bloxham
Managing Editor: Samantha Warrington
Editor: Anna Southgate
Assistant Editor: Jo Morley
Pattern Checker: Joanna Benner
Designer: Blanche Williams at Harper Williams Ltd
Photographer: Becky Joiner, Simon Pask
Chart Illustrator: Stephen Dew
Models: Samantha Warrington, Mollie Budden, Fred Williams
Shoot assistant: Amy Morris
Project images shot on location at:
The Old Farmhouse, Somerset (01823 674567)
Production Manager: Rohana Yusof

9 8 7 6 5 4 3 2 1
Printed in China by Hung Hing

Contents

Introduction

Born of a necessity to provide warm, durable clothing, knitting techniques and traditions have passed from one generation to the next, and from country to country during the course of many centuries. Consequently we can see the influence of various cultures in the stitches that we use today.

I developed a keen interest in traditional knitting while living in Aberdeen, in Scotland, several years ago. Many of my neighbors wore beautiful hand-knitted Fair Isle sweaters, some of which were several years old and yet looked as fresh as new. One neighbor also regularly wore a hap shawl around her shoulders. The women had made all of these garments themselves, without relying on printed patterns, but using traditional motifs and stitches that they had learned from their mothers. Naturally each of these mothers had learned the patterns from their mothers before them.

I was so taken with the Fair Isle sweaters that I set about learning how to take the familiar motifs and add my own choice of colors. It took a while to master the technique, but I am pleased to say that I gradually improved. I also learned to make delicate Shetland lace shawls and created one of my own while I was expecting my son.

Currently living in northeast Norfolk, in England, I have had the opportunity to study, at close hand, some traditional fishermen's ganseys. Frequent visits to the museums of Cromer and Sheringham—both of which have collections and

ABOVE: *Scottish herring girls knit while they wait for the fishing boats to arrive. They are making socks, and are knitting in the round using double-pointed needles.*

information on these fascinating pieces—stimulated my interest and I have since collected numerous examples of the stitches used, many of which feature in the following pages. Of course, my experience is with traditional knitting styles and techniques from around the British Isles, but similar traditions can be found throughout the world, and many of them are included in this book.

Knitting: A Brief History

Although it seems certain that knitting originated in the Middle East, perhaps in the 11th century, it has an elusive history. Weaving probably came first, as this would have been a fairly easy technique to develop without the need for any equipment other than the fingers. Fibers were made by twisting and stretching stems together. These fibers, usually flax, could then be woven together to produce fabric. There are many depictions of weaving looms in the tombs of ancient Egypt. Some of the earliest fragments of this fabric were produced in the Middle East, and drop spindles for spinning cotton and flax have been found dating back to 3000 BCE.

EUROPEAN TRENDS

It is largely thanks to Mediterranean trade routes that knitting traveled from the Middle East to Europe, primarily through Spain, where the earliest pieces were made for wealthy patrons or the Church. From Spain, knitting traditions spread further across Europe, with significant traditions evolving in France, Italy, Austria, Germany, and Scandinavia. Knitting grew to be an important part of the economy in many of these countries, and it was not long before knitting guilds were established in order to protect and maintain the standard of work that had developed over the years.

On a domestic level, various countries began to specialize in different techniques, and these are the primary focus of this book. Austria and Germany favored cabled fabrics decorated with colorful embroidery, for example, while Scandinavian countries developed distinctive designs using two-stranded knitting, either in a color or as a textured pattern. Stockings and hats were a familiar commodity in France and Italy, while Scotland and Ireland became known respectively for intricate decorative patterns and cables.

Many of these traditions developed because of the way in which knitting was done at the time—on a circular frame rather than with two needles. When knitting "in the round," as the technique was known, the knitter always had the same side of the work facing him or her. It was easy, therefore to develop a wide range of repeating textured patterns like those used for the fishermen's ganseys that I have seen in Norfolk, and for which there are similar traditions all around the North Sea coasts and the Eastern seaboard of North America.

Everyday pieces of knitting were made for practical reasons; as they wore out they would be discarded. For the most part, they were made from perishable fibers, such as cotton, flax, or wool. Cotton was first cultivated in Asia and South America and there are some early fragments of socks knitted with cotton dyed using natural plant materials. Flax is thought to have been cultivated long before this in and around the Mediterranean. The most commonly used fiber in northern Europe was sheep wool. All of these fibers were spun by hand at first, and this was a job allocated to the women. Other fibers, such as silk, hemp, and nettles were used occasionally, but silk, imported from China, was only for the very wealthy.

With developing trade, Germany exported what was then known as Saxony wool; a fine soft merino wool, which was much more pleasant to knit with than the more coarse wool used for stockings and workwear. This yarn also took well to dyeing and the wide range of colors that became available may have encouraged more people to take up knitting, and to produce a wider range of clothing and what we might now call accessories; shawls, socks, petticoats, and some babywear.

TRENDS IN THE UNITED STATES

From early in the 19th century, knitting began to gain popularity in the English drawing room and, subsequently, in the American colonies. The knitting of stockings had been widespread in the 17th century, often paid for in tobacco rather than cash. Scottish knitters had for many years been "paid" under a similar system known as the Truck system. A merchant would supply the wool and the knitter would be paid for the work in the form of goods from the merchant's shop, usually tea or soap, or sometimes cloth. The Governor of Virginia in 1662 offered ten pounds of tobacco for every dozen stockings, but with the advent of the stocking frame in the mid-18th century, this trade was no longer economic and knitting was undertaken more for pleasure than payment. Pieces we would now call household items were most popular, used for decorative rather than utility purposes. The families that emigrated to America would carry their

ABOVE: *A mother steals a glance from her knitting to admire her children in this ideal of family life in colonial America.*
LEFT: *Influenced by the fine lace of 18th-century Venice, exquisite table mats and doilies feature in a number of domestic knitting traditions from the United States to Estonia.*

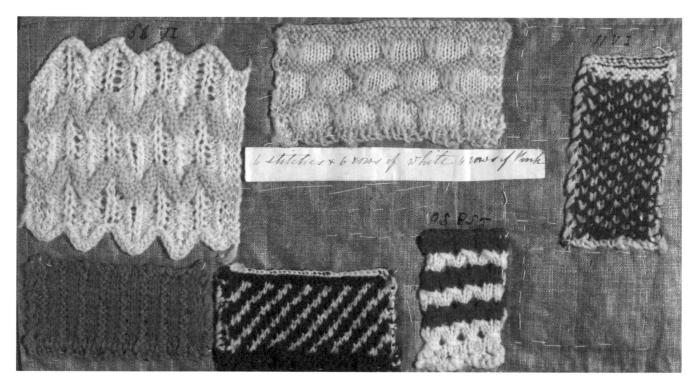

traditions with them and so this country shows more influences than any other; Viennese lace doilies, Aran throws, and whitework counterpanes were among the favorite knitted items in 19th-century colonial homes.

Using This Book

Organized by stitch type, this book features patterns and projects using six main types of knitting stitch. All of them have stood the test of time since they were first used, often centuries ago, in many countries of the world. The groups are Textured Stitches, Twisted Stitches, Raised Stitches, Cable Stitches, Lace Stitches, and Colorwork.

I have chosen designs that crop up in more than one culture, even though they may feature more traditionally in a different form of textile. For example the tree of life appears in many guises in knitting—in textured work, traveling stitches, and colorwork. But it also crops up in other textiles from time to time—for example in cross-stitch embroidery from Europe or carpets of the Middle East. They may have been passed from one group of people to another via trade routes or they may have occurred spontaneously as knitters developed their skills. What is evident is that these ancient stitches have traveled the world over time, handed down from

one generation to the next, and adapted to suit different lifestyles, needs, and cultural trends.

Knitting stitches form a grid when placed together—sometimes square and sometimes rectangular—and this determines the shape of a colored or textured motif. There is no limit to the designs that can be produced, especially where a fine yarn and small needles are used. Even curved shapes can be achieved, as can be seen in the beautifully elaborate pictorial representations of birds and plants of Dutch brocade knitting and the snowflake designs of Norway and the Shetland Islands. Geometric designs, when placed beside or above and below one another, often tessellate to create new, intermediate shapes, so that any pattern with four lines of symmetry will work as an allover design. Cross shapes are popular patterns in knitting for exactly this reason.

Over 150 traditional patterns feature in this book, along with 12 projects that use a number of them, or variations of them. The selection allows you to make the projects using a range of different stitches. Choose those with the same stitch count to begin with, but as you become more proficient, adapt the patterns to your own choice of motif. You could also design a piece entirely from scratch by selecting one or more

ABOVE: *A page from a sample book dating from the mid-19th century. Among the samples are some pieces of solid wool knitting, of undyed Shetland wool and of colored knitting.*

of the motifs to create something completely unique.

YARN CHOICES

For all of the knitted swatches, I have chosen to use wool produced by the Natural Fibre Company in Cornwall, in an attempt to replicate the characteristics of the pieces as they would have been made in the past. Sheep and goats were domesticated in many areas and their wool could be spun using a drop spindle —a very simple tool of a pin, or stick, with a weight on the end. Depending on the skill of the spinner and the breed of sheep, yarn could be produced from the finest weights for knitting lace to chunky thicknesses suitable for blankets.

Wool is an ideal material for colored motifs, as it is slightly hairy and causes the strands to stick together, which is useful when joining in new colors. While the finest wools tend to be used for lacework, and cables show up best using smooth yarns in pale colors, there is no reason why you could not substitute yarns of your choice for any one of the projects given here.

Chapter One
TEXTURED STITCHES

Textured knitting stitches are among the world's oldest, having originated in southern Europe during the late-16th century. Many of these stitches also happen to be the widest traveled. Featuring prolifically in the knitting traditions of several countries, they continue to be well known—and used—today. Age-old favorites, such as basketweaves, ladders, zigzags, diamonds, crosses, and hearts offer a relatively easy way of giving single-color knitted fabrics a richer, more interesting decorative finish.

Knit and Purl

The "discovery" of the purl stitch, at the turn of the 17th century, set knitting on a path of great innovation. Introducing the concept of textured stitches, it meant that fabrics could be created with all manner of subtle patterning, featuring repeated shapes and motifs laden with symbolism.

Before the 17th century, all knitting was done in the round. The result was a fabric of uniform texture, with a knit stitch on the right side, and what became known as a purl stitch on the wrong side. Commonly referred to as stockinette stitch, the technique produced pieces without a single raised stitch on the right side of the work.

Early Textured Knitting

The earliest known example of a purl stitch is found on a pair of stockings from the tomb of Eleanora di Toledo, who died in 1562. The pattern around the top of the stockings employs a few rows of trellis diamonds and is similar to those on the nightshirt said to have been worn by King Charles I on the day of his execution in 1649. It is assumed, therefore, that the purl stitch came into use early in the 17th century.

Once it was discovered how to make the ridge on the right side, by working the stitch with the yarn at the front of the needles, it was used to form textured patterns, known as brocade. Some of the designs were extremely elaborate, taking the form of birds or flowers, but these garments were only for the wealthy. The purl stitch was also used to create geometric damask-type patterns on the cotton vests or undershirts (*nattroje*) of Danish men and women. Again, such pieces often featured diamonds and eight-pointed stars. In Italy silk stockings with patterned tops, akin to the King Charles brocade stitch on page 23, were popular, while fine silk stockings with textured clocks from calf to ankle were being made in France.

Domestic Developments

As knitting traditions spread across Europe from the late-18th century, the use of textured stitches became popular

ABOVE: *An early 18th-century Dutch petticoat, knitted in white, 2-ply cotton. The representations of birds and leaves are depicted in knit and purl stitches alone.*

within rural communities. This gave rise to a number of designs that were based on things seen in the countryside, such as hen's footprints, the ridges and furrows of the fields, or trees. In fact, the tree of life on page 22 is a familiar symbol that crops up in all cultures and in all kinds of crafts, as does the six-pointed star on page 23, also known as the Norwegian star (see also, page 118).

Textured patterns have become particularly associated with the geometric shapes seen on fishermen's sweaters from around the North Sea coasts. The fact that many of the stitches are geometric has allowed them to take on sea-faring symbolism and a number of them are said to represent rigging, fishing nets, pennants, and herringbones, among other things. Larger motifs show anchors

and stars. Variations on several themes can be seen in the knitting traditions of towns and villages all around the coasts of Scandinavia and the Netherlands, as well as Britain. Fishermen traveled beyond their own countries and stitch patterns from one locality were often picked up and copied by skilled knitters in other regions. In some places, knitting was a valuable means of income for many women and they weren't at all keen to have their ideas copied. Even today there are families who won't allow their ganseys to be photographed.

THE GANSEY TRADITION

The gansey tradition has continued down through many centuries as practical and serviceable workwear. Fishermen could spend many months at sea, sometimes in extreme temperatures and needed something warm and hardwearing. The basic gansey shape is the same whatever its country of origin. It is loose and square to allow freedom of movement and ease of repair.

The type of yarn and the mode of working make these garments ideal: the combinations of knit and purl stitches means that the loops lie in different directions, so trapping more air. A gansey is traditionally knitted in navy 5-ply wool on fine needles with about 12 stitches and 20 rounds to 1in (2.5cm). Stitches are often cast on with the yarn doubled to give a firmer edge. Sometimes the welts are split at the sides but then the knitting is continued in the round as far as the armholes so that there are no seams to come undone, often with a purl stitch used to mark the position where the seams would be. Stitches are increased either side of this "seam" after about 12in (30cm) to form an underarm gusset, which eliminates any "pull" on this area, essential in a garment that would be used every day for demanding work.

There is little, if any, neck shaping but straps are often added at the shoulders to give extra width, sometimes continuing down the sleeves. The sleeves are worked from the top downwards in order to facilitate repair when the salt water and general wear and tear cause them to fray. The areas across the chest and upper arms were often intricately patterned to keep the fisherman warm, as the patterned area produced a thicker texture.

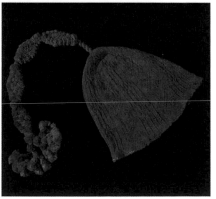

TOP: *A group of fisherman from Sheringham pose for a photograph in their hand-knitted ganseys. Traditionally a fisherman would have two ganseys—one for working in and one for Sunday best.*

ABOVE: *This hand-knitted silk cap is thought to have been made in Spain during the 18th century. A textured pattern of chevrons and lozenges tapers towards the crown.*

Textured Stitches

Most textured stitches are known internationally. At their simplest, they are variations of moss stitch, which alternates stitches, or stockinette stitch, which alternates rows. Others are more elaborate, adopting familiar motifs, such as ladders, stars, and anchors. Often knitted in the round, many of them follow a natural progression, for example a diamond shape or a zigzag, which can be fitted into a variable number of stitches and changed to suit the size of the piece being made.

Pillar

Round 1: K4.
Round 2: P4.
Round 3: P4.
Round 4: K4.
Round 5: K4.
Round 6: P2, k2.
Round 7: P2, k2.
Round 8: K4.
Round 9: K4.
Round 10: P2, k2.
Round 11: P2, k2.
Round 12: K4.
Round 13: K4.
Round 14: P4.
Round 15: P4.
Round 16: P4.

Basketweave

Row 1: K7, (p1, k1) x 3, p1.
Row 2: (K1, p1) x 3, k1, p7.
Row 3: P8, (k1, p1) x 3.
Row 4: (K1, p1) x 3, k1, p7.
Row 5: K7, (p1, k1) x 3, p1.
Row 6: (K1, p1) x 3, k8.
Row 7: K7, (p1, k1) x 3, p1.
Row 8: (K1, p1) x 3, k1, p7.
Row 9: P8, (k1, p1) x 3.
Row 10: (K1, p1) x 3, k1, p7.
Row 11: K7, (p1, k1) x 3, p1.
Row 12: P7, (k1, p1) x 3, k1.
Row 13: (P1, k1) x 3, p1, k7.
Row 14: K8, (p1, k1) x 3.
Row 15: (P1, k1) x 3, p1, k7.
Row 16: P7, (k1, p1) x 3, k1.
Row 17: (P1, k1) x 3, p8.
Row 18: P7, (k1, p1) x 3, k1.
Row 19: (P1, k1) x 3, p1, k7.
Row 20: K8, (p1, k1) x 3.
Row 21: (P1, k1) x 3, p1, k7.
Row 22: P7, (k1, p1) x 3, k1.

Steps

Round 1: K4, p1, k1, p1, k3.
Round 2: K4, p3, k3.
Round 3: K4, p1, k1, p1, k3.
Round 4: K4, p3, k3.
Round 5: K4, p1, k1, p1, k3.
Round 6: P10.
Round 7: (P1, k1) x 5.
Round 8: P10.
Round 9: K4, p1, k1, p1, k3.
Round 10: K4, p3, k3.
Round 11: K4, p1, k1, p1, k3.
Round 12: K4, p3, k3.

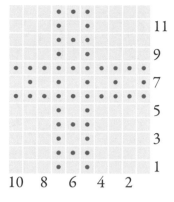

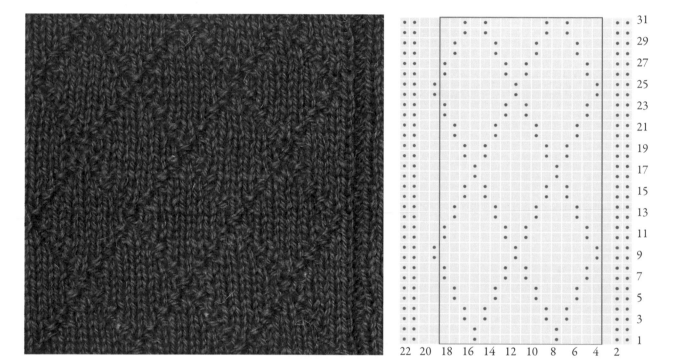

Net Mask

Round 1: P2, k1, * k4, p1, k7, p1, k3.
Rep from *, k2, p2.
Round 2: P2, k1, * k4, p1, k7, p1, k3.
Rep from *, k2, p2.
Round 3: P2, k1, * k3, p1, k1, p1, k5, p1, k1, p1, k2. Rep from *, k2, p2.
Round 4: P2, k1, * k3, p1, k1, p1, k5, p1, k1, p1, k2. Rep from *, k2, p2.
Round 5: P2, k1, * k2, (p1, k3) x 3, p1, k1.
Rep from *, k2, p2.
Round 6: P2, k1, * k2, (p1, k3) x 3, p1, k1.
Rep from *, k2, p2.
Round 7: P2, k1, * (k1, p1, k5, p1) x 2.
Rep from *, k2, p2.
Round 8: P2, k1, * (k1, p1, k5, p1) x 2.
Rep from *, k2, p2.
Round 9: P2, k1, * (p1, k7) x 2. Rep from *, p1, k1, p2.
Round 10: P2, k1, * (p1, k7) x 2. Rep from *, p1, k1, p2.
Round 11: P2, k1, * (k1, p1, k5, p1) x 2.

Rep from *, k2, p2.
Round 12: P2, k1, * (k1, p1, k5, p1) x 2.
Rep from *, k2, p2.
Round 13: P2, k1, * k2, (p1, k3) x 3, p1, k1.
Rep from *, k2, p2.
Round 14: P2, k1, * k2, (p1, k3) x 3, p1, k1.
Rep from *, k2, p2.
Round 15: P2, k1, * k3, p1, k1, p1, k5, p1, k1, p1, k2. Rep from *, k2, p2.
Round 16: P2, k1, * k3, p1, k1, p1, k5, p1, k1, p1, k2. Rep from *, k2, p2.
Round 17: P2, k1, * k4, p1, k7, p1, k3.
Rep from *, k2, p2.
Round 18: P2, k1, * k4, p1, k7, p1, k3.
Rep from *, k2, p2.
Round 19: P2, k1, * k3, p1, k1, p1, k5, p1, k1, p1, k2. Rep from *, k2, p2.
Round 20: P2, k1, * k3, p1, k1, p1, k5, p1, k1, p1, k2. Rep from *, k2, p2.
Round 21: P2, k1, * k2, (p1, k3) x 3, p1, k1.
Rep from *, k2, p2.
Round 22: P2, k1, * k2, (p1, k3) x 3, p1, k1.

Rep from *, k2, p2.
Round 23: P2, k1, * (k1, p1, k5, p1) x 2.
Rep from *, k2, p2.
Round 24: P2, k1, * (k1, p1, k5, p1) x 2.
Rep from *, k2, p2.
Round 25: P2, k1, * (p1, k7) x 2. Rep from *, p1, k1, p2.
Round 26: P2, k1, * (p1, k7) x 2. Rep from *, p1, k1, p2.
Round 27: P2, k1, * (k1, p1, k5, p1) x 2.
Rep from *, k2, p2.
Round 28: P2, k1, * (k1, p1, k5, p1) x 2.
Rep from *, k2, p2.
Round 29: P2, k1, * k2, (p1, k3) x 3, p1, k1.
Rep from *, k2, p2.
Round 30: P2, k1, * k2, (p1, k3) x 3, p1, k1.
Rep from *, k2, p2.
Round 31: P2, k1, * k3, p1, k1, p1, k5, p1, k1, p1, k2. Rep from *, k2, p2.
Round 32: P2, k1, * k3, p1, k1, p1, k5, p1, k1, p1, k2. Rep from *, k2, p2.

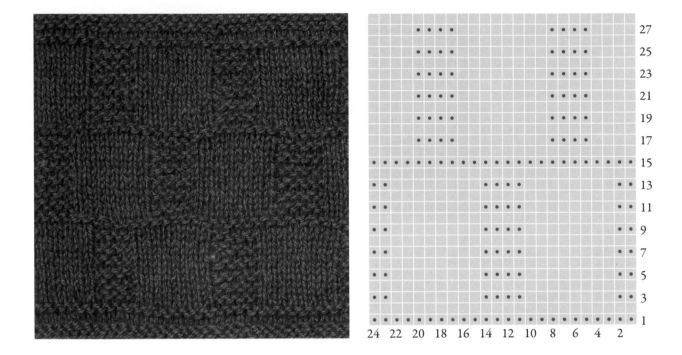

Vicar of Morwenstow
Round 1: P24.
Round 2: K24.
Round 3: P2, k8, p4, k8, p2.
Round 4: K24.
Round 5: P2, k8, p4, k8, p2.
Round 6: K24.
Round 7: P2, k8, p4, k8, p2.
Round 8: K24.
Round 9: P2, k8, p4, k8, p2.
Round 10: K24.

Round 11: P2, k8, p4, k8, p2.
Round 12: K24.
Round 13: P2, k8, p4, k8, p2.
Round 14: K24.
Round 15: P24.
Round 16: K24.
Round 17: K4, p4, k8, p4, k4.
Round 18: K24.
Round 19: K4, p4, k8, p4, k4.
Round 20: K24.
Round 21: K4, p4, k8, p4, k4.

Round 22: K24.
Round 23: K4, p4, k8, p4, k4.
Round 24: K24.
Round 25: K4, p4, k8, p4, k4.
Round 26: K24.
Round 27: K4, p4, k8, p4, k4.
Round 28: K24.

John Northcott
Multiple of 6
Round 1: P6, * p6. Rep from *, p6.
Round 2: K6, * k6. Rep from *, k6.
Round 3: K6, * k6. Rep from *, k6.
Round 4: K6, * k6. Rep from *, k6.
Round 5: P6, * p6. Rep from *, p6
Round 6: K6, * k6. Rep from *, k6.
Round 7: K6, * k6. Rep from *, k6.
Round 8: K6, * k6. Rep from *, k6.
Round 9: P6, * p6. Rep from *, p6.
Round 10: K6, * k6. Rep from *, k6.
Round 11: P3, k3, * p3, k3. Rep from *, p3, k3.
Round 12: K6, * k6. Rep from *, k6.
Round 13: P3, k3, * p3, k3. Rep from *, p3, k3.
Round 14: K6, * k6. Rep from *, k6.
Round 15: P3, k3, * p3, k3. Rep from *, p3, k3.
Round 16: K6, * k6. Rep from *, k6.
Round 17: P3, k3, * p3, k3. Rep from *, p3, k3.
Round 18: K6, * k6. Rep from *, k6.
Round 19: P3, k3, * p3, k3. Rep from *, p3, k3.

Round 20: K6, * k6. Rep from *, k6.
Round 21: P3, k3, * p3, k3. Rep from *, p3, k3.
Round 22: K6, * k6. Rep from *, k6.

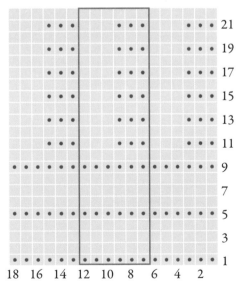

Robin Hood's Bay

Round 1: P2, k11.
Round 2: P2, k11.
Round 3: P2, k5, p1, k5.
Round 4: P2, k5, p1, k5.
Round 5: P2, k4, p1, k1, p1, k4.
Round 6: P2, k4, p1, k1, p1, k4.
Round 7: P2, k3, (p1, k1) x 2, p1, k3.
Round 8: P2, k3, (p1, k1) x 2, p1, k3.
Round 9: P2, k2, (p1, k1) x 3, p1, k2.
Round 10: P2, k2, (p1, k1) x 3, p1, k2.
Round 11: P2, (k1, p1) x 5, k1.
Round 12: P2, (k1, p1) x 5, k1.
Round 13: P2, k2, (p1, k1) x 3, p1, k2.
Round 14: P2, k2, (p1, k1) x 3, p1, k2.
Round 15: P2, k3, (p1, k1) x 2, p1, k3.
Round 16: P2, k3, (p1, k1) x 2, p1, k3.
Round 17: P2, k4, p1, k1, p1, k4.
Round 18: P2, k4, p1, k1, p1, k4.
Round 19: P2, k5, p1, k5.
Round 20: P2, k5, p1, k5.
Round 21: P2, k11.
Round 22: P2, k11.

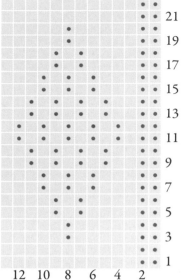

Zigzag

Round 1: (P1, k1) x 2, p1, k10, p1.
Round 2: P1, k2, p1, k1, p1, k9, p1.
Round 3: P1, k3, p1, k1, p1, k8, p1.
Round 4: P1, k4, p1, k1, p1, k7, p1.
Round 5: P1, k5, p1, k1, p1, k6, p1.
Round 6: P1, k6, p1, k1, p1, k5, p1.
Round 7: P1, k7, p1, k1, p1, k4, p1.
Round 8: P1, k8, p1, k1, p1, k3, p1.
Round 9: P1, k9, p1, k1, p1, k2, p1.
Round 10: P1, k10, (p1, k1) x 2, p1.
Round 11: P1, k9, p1, k1, p1, k2, p1.
Round 12: P1, k8, p1, k1, p1, k3, p1.
Round 13: P1, k7, p1, k1, p1, k4, p1.
Round 14: P1, k6, p1, k1, p1, k5, p1.
Round 15: P1, k5, p1, k1, p1, k6, p1.
Round 16: P1, k4, p1, k1, p1, k7, p1.
Round 17: P1, k3, p1, k1, p1, k8, p1.
Round 18: P1, k2, p1, k1, p1, k9, p1.
Round 19: (P1, k1) x 2, p1, k10, p1.
Round 20: P1, k2, p1, k1, p1, k9, p1.
Round 21: P1, k3, p1, k1, p1, k8, p1.
Round 22: P1, k4, p1, k1, p1, k7, p1.
Round 23: P1, k5, p1, k1, p1, k6, p1.
Round 24: P1, k6, p1, k1, p1, k5, p1.
Round 25: P1, k7, p1, k1, p1, k4, p1.
Round 26: P1, k8, p1, k1, p1, k3, p1.
Round 27: P1, k9, p1, k1, p1, k2, p1.
Round 28: P1, k10, (p1, k1) x 2, p1.
Round 29: P1, k9, p1, k1, p1, k2, p1.

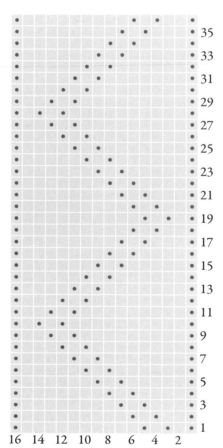

Round 30: P1, k8, p1, k1, p1, k3, p1.
Round 31: P1, k7, p1, k1, p1, k4, p1.
Round 32: P1, k6, p1, k1, p1, k5, p1.
Round 33: P1, k5, p1, k1, p1, k6, p1.
Round 34: P1, k4, p1, k1, p1, k7, p1.
Round 35: P1, k3, p1, k1, p1, k8, p1.
Round 36: P1, k2, p1, k1, p1, k9, p1.

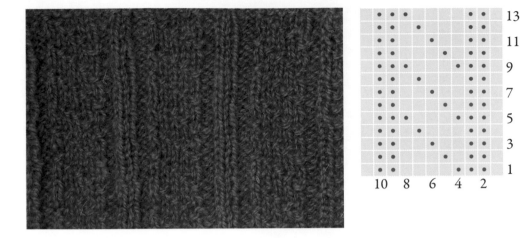

Tanker's Pattern

Round 1: K1, p3, k4, p2, k1.
Round 2: K1, p2, k1, p1, k3, p2, k1.
Round 3: K1, p2, k2, p1, k2, p2, k1.
Round 4: K1, p2, k3, p1, k1, p2, k1.
Round 5: K1, p3, k3, p3, k1.
Round 6: K1, p2, k1, p1, k3, p2, k1.
Round 7: K1, p2, k2, p1, k2, p2, k1.

Round 8: K1, p2, k3, p1, k1, p2, k1.
Round 9: K1, p3, k3, p3, k1.
Round 10: K1, p2, k1, p1, k3, p2, k1.
Round 11: K1, p2, k2, p1, k2, p2, k1.
Round 12: K1, p2, k3, p1, k1, p2, k1.
Round 13: K1, p2, k4, p3, k1.

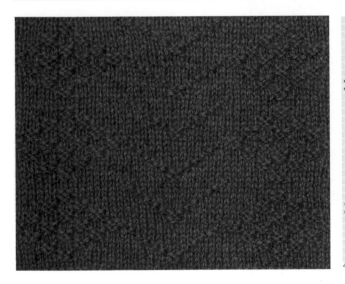

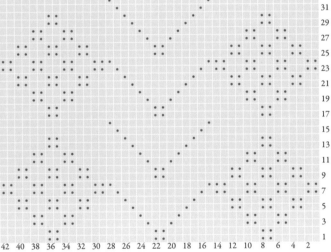

Tarr Bishop

Round 1: K6, (p2, k12) x 2, p2, k6.
Round 2: K6, (p2, k12) x 2, p2, k6.
Round 3: K4, p2, k2, p2, k9, p1, k2, p1, k9, p2, k2, p2, k4.
Round 4: K4, p2, k2, p2, k8, p1, k4, p1, k8, p2, k2, p2, k4.
Round 5: (K2, p2) x 3, k5, p1, k6, p1, k5, (p2, k2) x 3.
Round 6: (K2, p2) x 3, k4, p1, k8, p1, k4, (p2, k2) x 3.
Round 7: (P2, k2) x 3, p2, k1, p1, k10, p1, k1, (p2, k2) x 3, p2.
Round 8: (P2, k2) x 3, p3, k12, p3, (k2, p2) x 3.
Round 9: (K2, p2) x 3, k8, p2, k8, (p2, k2) x 3.
Round 10: (K2, p2) x 3, k8, p2, k8, (p2, k2) x 3.
Round 11: K4, p2, k2, p2, k9, p1, k2, p1, k9,

p2, k2, p2, k4.
Round 12: K4, p2, k2, p2, k8, p1, k4, p1, k8, p2, k2, p2, k4.
Round 13: K4, p1, k1, p2, k9, p1, k6, p1, k9, p2, k6.
Round 14: K6, p2, (k8, p1) x 2, k8, p2, k6.
Round 15: K15, p1, k10, p1, k15.
Round 16: K14, p1, k12, p1, k14.
Round 17: K6, (p2, k12) x 2, p2, k6.
Round 18: K6, (p2, k12) x 2, p2, k6.
Round 19: K4, p2, k2, p2, k9, p1, k2, p1, k9, p2, k2, p2, k4.
Round 20: K4, p2, k2, p2, k8, p1, k4, p1, k8, p2, k2, p2, k4.
Round 21: (K2, p2) x 3, k5, p1, k6, p1, k5, (p2, k2) x 3.
Round 22: (K2, p2) x 3, k4, p1, k8, p1, k4,

(p2, k2) x 3.
Round 23: (P2, k2) x 3, p2, k1, p1, k10, p1, k1, (p2, k2) x 3, p2.
Round 24: (P2, k2) x 3, p3, k12, p3, (k2, p2) x 3.
Round 25: (K2, p2) x 3, k8, p2, k8, (p2, k2) x 3.
Round 26: (K2, p2) x 3, k8, p2, k8, (p2, k2) x 3.
Round 27: K4, p2, k2, p2, k9, p1, k2, p1, k9, p2, k2, p2, k4.
Round 28: K4, p2, k2, p2, k8, p1, k4, p1, k8, p2, k2, p2, k4.
Round 29: K6, p2, k9, p1, k6, p1, k9, p2, k6.
Round 30: K6, p2, (k8, p1) x 2, k8, p2, k6.
Round 31: K15, p1, k10, p1, k15.
Round 32: K14, p1, k12, p1, k14.

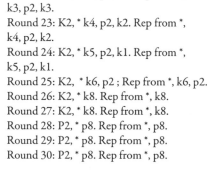

Herringbone

Round 1: P2, * p8. Rep from *, p8.
Round 2: P2, * p8. Rep from *, p8.
Round 3: P2, * p8. Rep from *, p8.
Round 4: K2, * k8. Rep from *, k8.
Round 5: P2, * k8. Rep from *, k8.
Round 6: K2, * k6, p2. Rep from *, k6, p2.
Round 7: K2, * k5, p2, k1. Rep from *, k5, p2, k1.
Round 8: K2, * k4, p2, k2. Rep from *, k4, p2, k2.
Round 9: K2, * k3, p2, k3. Rep from *, k3, p2, k3.
Round 10: K2, * k2, p2, k4.
Rep from *, k2, p2, k4.
Round 11: K2, * k1, p2, k5. Rep from *, k1, p2, k5.

Round 12: K2, * p2, k6. Rep from *, p2, k6.
Round 13: K1, p1, * p1, k6, p1. Rep from *, p1, k6, p1.
Round 14: P2, * k6, p2. Rep from *, k6, p2.
Round 15: P2, * p8. Rep from *, p8.
Round 16: P2, * p8. Rep from *, p8.
Round 17: P2, * k6, p2. Rep from *, k6, p2.
Round 18: K1, p1, * p1, k6, p1. Rep from *, p1, k6, p1.
Round 19: K2, * p2, k6. Rep from *, p2, k6.
Round 20: K2, * k1, p2, k5. Rep from *, k1, p2, k5.
Round 21: K2, * k2, p2, k4. Rep from *, k2, p2, k4.

Round 22: K2, * k3, p2, k3. Rep from *, k3, p2, k3.
Round 23: K2, * k4, p2, k2. Rep from *, k4, p2, k2.
Round 24: K2, * k5, p2, k1. Rep from *, k5, p2, k1.
Round 25: K2, * k6, p2 ; Rep from *, k6, p2.
Round 26: K2, * k8. Rep from *, k8.
Round 27: K2, * k8. Rep from *, k8.
Round 28: P2, * p8. Rep from *, p8.
Round 29: P2, * p8. Rep from *, p8.
Round 30: P2, * p8. Rep from *, p8.

Northwest Scotland

Round 1: P1, k4, p2, k4, p1.
Round 2: (P2, k4) x 2.
Round 3: K1, p2, k4, p2, k3.
Round 4: K2, p2, k4, p2, k2.
Round 5: K3, p2, k4, p2, k1.
Round 6: (K4, p2) x 2.

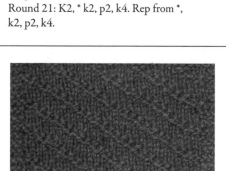

Scottish Half Flag

Round 1: K1, p5.
Round 2: K2, p4.
Round 3: K3, p3.
Round 4: K4, p2.
Round 5: K5, p1.
Round 6: K1, p5.
Round 7: K2, p4.
Round 8: K3, p3.
Round 9: K4, p2.
Round 10: K5, p1.
Round 11: K1, p5.
Round 12: K2, p4.
Round 13: K3, p3.
Round 14: K4, p2.
Round 15: K5, p1.

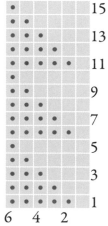

Eriksay Hearts

Round 1: K1, p2, k13, p2, k1.
Round 2: K1, p2, k6, p1, k6, p2, k1.
Round 3: K1, p2, k6, p1, k6, p2, k1.
Round 4: K1, p2, k5, p1, k1, p1, k5, p2, k1.
Round 5: K1, p2, k5, p1, k1, p1, k5, p2, k1.
Round 6: K1, p2, k4, (p1, k1) x 2, p1, k4, p2, k1.
Round 7: K1, p2, k4, (p1, k1) x 2, p1, k4, p2, k1.
Round 8: K1, p2, k3, (p1, k1) x 3, p1, k3, p2, k1.
Round 9: K1, p2, k3, (p1, k1) x 3, p1, k3, p2, k1.
Round 10: K1, p2, k2, p1, k1, p1, k3, p1, k1, p1, k2, p2, k1.
Round 11: K1, p2, k2, p1, k1, p1, k3, p1, k1, p1, k2, p2, k1.
Round 12: K1, p2, (k1, p1) x 2, k5, (p1, k1) x 2, p2, k1.
Round 13: K1, p2, (k1, p1) x 2, k5, (p1, k1)

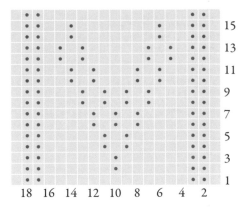

x 2, p2, k1. Round 14: K1, p2, k2, p1, k7, p1, k2, p2, k1.
Round 15: K1, p2, k2, p1, k7, p1, k2, p2, k1.
Round 16: K1, p2, k13, p2, k1.

Boddam

Round 1: P2, (k2, p1) x 3, k6.
Round 2: P2, (k2, p1) x 3, k6.
Round 3: P2, k3, (p1, k2) x 2, p1, k5.
Round 4: P2, k3, (p1, k2) x 2, p1, k5.
Round 5: P2, k4, (p1, k2) x 2, p1, k4.
Round 6: P2, k4, (p1, k2) x 2, p1, k4.
Round 7: P2, k5, (p1, k2) x 2, p1, k3.
Round 8: P2, k5, (p1, k2) x 2, p1, k3.
Round 9: P2, k6, (p1, k2) x 3.
Round 10: P2, k6, (p1, k2) x 3.
Round 11: P2, k7, (p1, k2) x 2, p1, k1.
Round 12: P2, k7, (p1, k2) x 2, p1, k1.
Round 13: P2, k6, p1, k2, p2, k1, p1, k2.
Round 14: P2, k6, (p1, k2) x 3.
Round 15: P2, k5, (p1, k2) x 2, p1, k3.
Round 16: P2, k5, (p1, k2) x 2, p1, k3.
Round 17: P2, k4, (p1, k2) x 2, p1, k4.
Round 18: P2, k4, (p1, k2) x 2, p1, k4.
Round 19: P2, k3, (p1, k2) x 2, p1, k5.
Round 20: P2, k3, (p1, k2) x 2, p1, k5.
Round 21: P2, (k2, p1) x 3, k6.

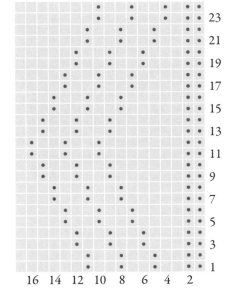

Round 22: P2, (k2, p1) x 3, k6.
Round 23: P2, k1, (p1, k2) x 2, p1, k7.
Round 24: P2, k1, (p1, k2) x 2, p1, k7.

Married Fishermen

Row 1: (P1, k1) x 2, p1, k3, p1, k10.
Row 2: P9, k1, p3, k1, p2, k3.
Row 3: P1, k1, (p1, k3) x 2, p1, k8.
Row 4: P7, k1, p3, k1, p4, k3.
Row 5: P1, k1, p1, k5, p1, k3, p1, k6.
Row 6: P5, k1, p3, k1, p6, k3.
Row 7: P1, k1, p1, k7, p1, k3, p1, k4.
Row 8: (P3, k1) x 2, p8, k3.
Row 9: P1, k1, p1, k9, p1, k3, p1, k2.
Row 10: P1, k1, p3, k1, p10, k3.
Row 11: P1, k1, p1, k9, p1, k3, p1, k2.
Row 12: (P3, k1) x 2, p8, k3.
Row 13: P1, k1, p1, k7, p1, k3, p1, k4.
Row 14: P5, k1, p3, k1, p6, k3.
Row 15: P1, k1, p1, k5, p1, k3, p1, k6.
Row 16: P7, k1, p3, k1, p4, k3.

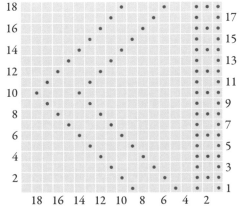

Row 17: P1, k1, (p1, k3) x 2, p1, k8.
Row 18: P9, k1, p3, k1, p2, k3.

Diamond Border

Round 1: P6, k6.
Round 2: P6, k6.
Round 3: P5, k1, p1, k5.
Round 4: P5, k1, p1, k5.
Round 5: P4, (k1, p1) x 2, k4.
Round 6: P4, (k1, p1) x 2, k4.
Round 7: P3, (k1, p1) x 3, k3.
Round 8: P3, (k1, p1) x 3, k3.
Round 9: P2, (k1, p1) x 4, k2.
Round 10: P2, (k1, p1) x 4, k2.
Round 11: (P1, k1) x 6.
Round 12: (P1, k1) x 6.
Round 13: P2, (k1, p1) x 4, k2.
Round 14: P2, (k1, p1) x 4, k2.
Round 15: P3, (k1, p1) x 3, k3.
Round 16: P3, (k1, p1) x 3, k3.

Round 17: P4, (k1, p1) x 2, k4.
Round 18: P4, (k1, p1) x 2, k4.
Round 19: P5, k1, p1, k5.
Round 20: P5, k1, p1, k5.

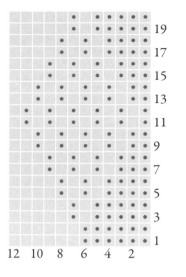

Mallaig Diamond

Round 1: P1, k1, (p1, k6) x 2.
Round 2: P3, k6, p1, k6.
Round 3: (P1, k1, p1, k5) x 2.
Round 4: P3, k5, p1, k1, p1, k5.
Round 5: P1, k1, p1, k4, (p1, k1) x 2, p1, k4.
Round 6: P3, k4, (p1, k1) x 2, p1, k4.
Round 7: P1, k1, p1, k3, (p1, k1) x 2, p1, k1, p1, k3.
Round 8: P3, k3, (p1, k1) x 3, p1, k3.
Round 9: P1, k1, p1, k2, p1, k1, p1, k3, p1, k1, p1, k2.
Round 10: P3, k2, p1, k1, p1, k3, p1, k1, p1, k2.
Round 11: (P1, k1) x 3, p1, k5, (p1, k1) x 2.
Round 12: P3, (k1, p1) x 2, k5, (p1, k1) x 2.
Round 13: P1, k1, p1, k2, p1, k1, p1, k3, p1, k1, p1, k2.
Round 14: P3, k2, p1, k1, p1, k3, p1, k1, p1, k2.
Round 15: P1, k1, p1, k3, (p1, k1) x 2, p1, k1, p1, k3.
Round 16: P3, k3, (p1, k1) x 3, p1, k3.
Round 17: P1, k1, p1, k4, (p1, k1) x 2, p1, k4.
Round 18: P3, k4, (p1, k1) x 2, p1, k4.
Round 19: (P1, k1, p1, k5) x 2.
Round 20: P3, k5, p1, k1, p1, k5.

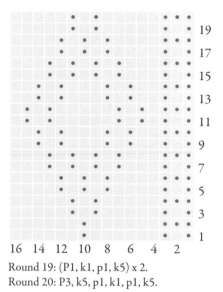

St Andrew's Cross

Row 1: K1, p1, k1, p9, k1, p1, k1.
Row 2: P1, k1, p1, k9, p1, k1, p1.
Row 3: (P1, k1) x 2, p7, (k1, p1) x 2.
Row 4: (K1, p1) x 2, k7, (p1, k1) x 2.
Row 5: P2, k1, p1, k1, p5, k1, p1, k1, p2.
Row 6: K2, p1, k1, p1, k5, p1, k1, p1, k2.
Row 7: (P3, k1, p1, k1) x 2, p3.
Row 8: (K3, p1, k1, p1) x 2, k3.
Row 9: P4, (k1, p1) x 3, k1, p4.
Row 10: K4, (p1, k1) x 3, p1, k4.
Row 11: P5, (k1, p1) x 2, k1, p5.
Row 12: K5, (p1, k1) x 2, p1, k5.
Row 13: P6, k1, p1, k1, p6.
Row 14: K6, p1, k1, p1, k6.
Row 15: P5, (k1, p1) x 2, k1, p5.
Row 16: K5, (p1, k1) x 2, p1, k5.
Row 17: P4, (k1, p1) x 3, k1, p4.
Row 18: K4, (p1, k1) x 3, p1, k4.
Row 19: (P3, k1, p1, k1) x 2, p3.
Row 20: (K3, p1, k1, p1) x 2, k3.

Row 21: P2, k1, p1, k1, p5, k1, p1, k1, p2.
Row 22: K2, p1, k1, p1, k5, p1, k1, p1, k2.
Row 23: (P1, k1) x 2, p7, (k1, p1) x 2.
Row 24: (K1, p1) x 2, k7, (p1, k1) x 2.
Row 25: K1, p1, k1, p9, k1, p1, k1.
Row 26: P1, k1, p1, k9, p1, k1, p1.k2.

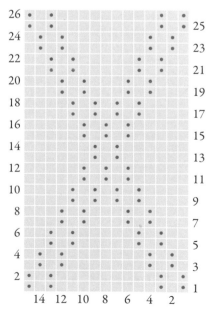

Anchor

Row 1: K15.
Row 2: P15.
Row 3: K7, p1, k7.
Row 4: P6, k3, p6.
Row 5: K5, (p1, k1) x 2, p1, k5.
Row 6: P4, k1, p1, k3, p1, k1, p4.
Row 7: K3, (p1, k1) x 4, p1, k3.
Row 8: P2, k1, p1, (k1, p2) x 2, k1, p1, k1, p2.
Row 9: (K1, p1) x 2, (k3, p1) x 2, k1, p1, k1.
Row 10: P2, k1, p1, k1, p2, k1, p4, k1, p2.
Row 11: K1, p1, k5, p1, k1, p1, k3, p1, k1.
Row 12: P6, k2, p7.
Row 13: K7, p1, k7.
Row 14: P7, k2, p6.
Row 15: K5, p1, k1, p1, k7.
Row 16: P7, k1, p2, k1, p4.
Row 17: (K3, p1) x 2, k7.
Row 18: P7, k1, p2, k1, p4.
Row 19: K5, p1, k1, p1, k7.
Row 20: P7, k2, p6.
Row 21: K7, p1, k7.
Row 22: P7, k1, p7.
Row 23: K7, p1, k7.
Row 24: P4, k7, p4.

Row 25: K7, p1, k7.
Row 26: P6, k1, p1, k1, p6.
Row 27: K5, p1, k3, p1, k5.
Row 28: P6, k1, p1, k1, p6.
Row 29: K7, p1, k7.
Row 30: P15.
Row 31: K15.

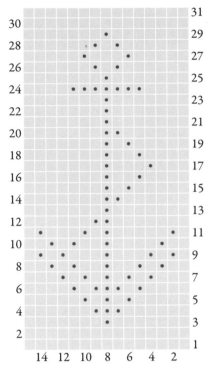

Tree of Life

Row 1: K7, p1, k1, p1, k7.
Row 2: P6, k2, p1, k2, p6.
Row 3: K5, p2, k3, p2, k5.
Row 4: P4, k2, p5, k2, p4.
Row 5: K3, p2, k2, p1, k1, p1, k2, p2, k3.
Row 6: (P2, k2) x 2, p1, (k2, p2) x 2.
Row 7: K1, p2, k2, p2, k3, p2, k2, p2, k1.
Row 8: K2, p2, k2, p5, k2, p2, k2.
Row 9: P1, k2, p2, k2, p1, k1, p1, k2, p2, k2, p1.
Row 10: (P2, k2) x 2, p1, (k2, p2) x 2.
Row 11: K1, p2, k2, p2, k3, p2, k2, p2, k1.
Row 12: P1, k1, p2, k2, p5, k2, p2, k1, p1.
Row 13: K3, p2, k2, p1, k1, p1, k2, p2, k3.
Row 14: (P2, k2) x 2, p1, (k2, p2) x 2.
Row 15: K2, p1, k2, p2, k3, p2, k2, p1, k2.
Row 16: P4, k2, p5, k2, p4.
Row 17: K3, p2, k2, p1, k1, p1, k2, p2, k3.
Row 18: P3, k1, p2, k2, p1, k2, p2, k1, p3.
Row 19: K5, p2, k3, p2, k5.
Row 20: P4, k2, p5, k2, p4.
Row 21: K4, p1, k2, p1, k1, p1, k2, p1, k4.
Row 22: P6, k2, p1, k2, p6.
Row 23: K5, p2, k3, p2, k5.
Row 24: (P5, k1) x 2, p5.

Row 25: K7, p1, k1, p1, k7.
Row 26: P6, k2, p1, k2, p6.
Row 27: K6, p1, k3, p1, k6.
Row 28: P17.
Row 29: K7, p1, k1, p1, k7.
Row 30: P7, k1, p1, k1, p7.
Row 31: K17.

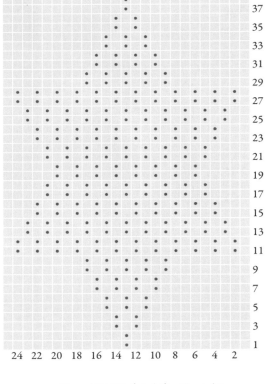

Humber Star

Round 1: K12, p1, k12.
Round 2: K12, p1, k12.
Round 3: K11, p1, k1, p1, k11.
Round 4: K11, p1, k1, p1, k11.
Round 5: K10, (p1, k1) x 2, p1, k10.
Round 6: K10, (p1, k1) x 2, p1, k10.
Round 7: K9, (p1, k1) x 3, p1, k9.
Round 8: K9, (p1, k1) x 2, p1, k11.
Round 9: K8, (p1, k1) x 4, p1, k8.
Round 10: K8, (p1, k1) x 4, p1, k8.
Round 11: (K1, p1) x 12, k1.
Round 12: (K1, p1) x 12, k1.

Round 13: K2, (p1, k1) x 10, p1, k2.
Round 14: K2, (p1, k1) x 10, p1, k2.
Round 15: K3, (p1, k1) x 9, p1, k3.
Round 16: K3, (p1, k1) x 9, p1, k3.
Round 17: K4, (p1, k1) x 8, p1, k4.
Round 18: K4, (p1, k1) x 8, p1, k4.
Round 19: K5, (p1, k1) x 7, p1, k5.
Round 20: K5, (p1, k1) x 7, p1, k5.
Round 21: K4, (p1, k1) x 8, p1, k4.
Round 22: K4, (p1, k1) x 8, p1, k4.
Round 23: K3, (p1, k1) x 9, p1, k3.
Round 24: K3, (p1, k1) x 9, p1, k3.
Round 25: K2, (p1, k1) x 10, p1, k2.

Round 26: K2, (p1, k1) x 10, p1, k2.
Round 27: (K1, p1) x 12, k1.
Round 28: (K1, p1) x 12, k1.
Round 29: K8, (p1, k1) x 4, p1, k8.
Round 30: K8, (p1, k1) x 4, p1, k8.
Round 31: K9, (p1, k1) x 3, p1, k9.
Round 32: K9, (p1, k1) x 3, p1, k9.
Round 33: K10, (p1, k1) x 2, p1, k10.
Round 34: K10, (p1, k1) x 2, p1, k10.
Round 35: K11, p1, k1, p1, k11.
Round 36: K11, p1, k1, p1, k11.
Round 37: K12, p1, k12.
Round 38: K12, p1, k12.

King Charles Brocade

Round 1: P20.
Round 2: P20.
Round 3: K20.
Round 4: P20.
Round 5: P20.
Round 6: K20.
Round 7: (K9, p1) x 2.
Round 8: (P1, k7, p1, k1) x 2.
Round 9: K1, p1, k5, p1, k3, p1, k5, p1, k2.
Round 10: K2, p1, k3, p1, k5, (p1, k3) x 2.
Round 11: K3, p1, k1, p1, k7, p1, k1, p1, k4.
Round 12: K4, p1, k9, p1, k5.
Round 13: K3, p1, k1, p1, k7, p1, k1, p1, k4.
Round 14: K2, p1, k3, p1, k5, (p1, k3) x 2.
Round 15: K1, p1, k5, p1, k3, p1, k5, p1, k2.
Round 16: (P1, k7, p1, k1) x 2.

Round 17: (K9, p1) x 2.
Round 18: K20.
Round 19: P20.
Round 20: P20.
Round 21: K20.
Round 22: P20.
Round 23: P20.

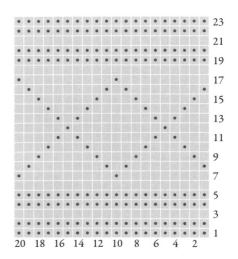

23

Eriksay Tote Bag

This design is based on the wonderfully intricate patterns found on an Eriksay gansey, and include Eriksay hearts and the tree of life (see pages 20 and 22). While these garments tend to be patterned all over, specific, individual, motifs are usually centered on the front and back. These patterns have been passed down from mother to daughter and knitted for many years. Traditionally they would often feature a tree of life and, probably, zigzags or a line of diamonds.

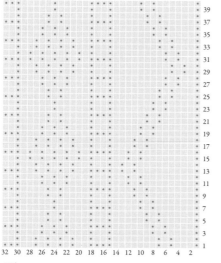

Chart 1

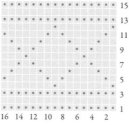

Chart 2

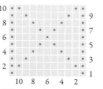

Chart 4

Size
The bag measures approximately 8⅔ x 13¾in (22 x 35cm)

Materials
4 x 1¾oz (50g) balls pink DK yarn
Size 6 (4mm) 16in (40cm) circular needle
2 wooden bag handles
Stitch holders

Gauge
Not important for this project

The bag is worked in the round from the bottom upwards.
Cast on 128 sts and join in the round, being careful not to twist sts.
Purl 1 round, then work Chart 1, repeating it four times around.
After 40 rounds have been worked, work Chart 2, increasing 3 sts evenly across last round.
Work Chart 3 for 40 rounds.
Work garter stitch for 5 rounds.

PLACE STRAPS FOR HANDLES
Bind off 14 sts, p10 (11 sts on needle), and work Chart 4 until strap measures approximately 4¾in (12cm).
Purl 1 row and leave sts on holder.
Rejoin yarn, bind off 19 sts, p10 (11 sts on needle) and work other strap to match.
Leave on holder.
Bind off 26 sts.

FINISHING
Slip straps through handles, bind off sts of second strap with next 11 sts of bag, bind off 19 sts, bind off sts of first strap with next 11 sts of bag.
Bind off rem sts.
Sew bottom (cast-on) edges of bag together.

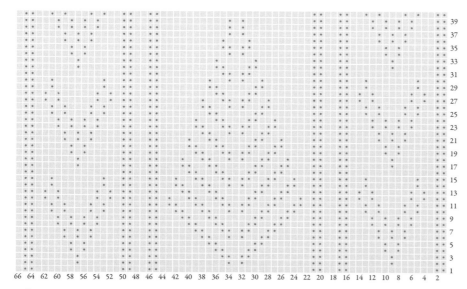

Chart 3

Hot Water Bottle Cover

The pattern on this hot water bottle cover is taken directly from an old Sheringham gansey, and is known as Tarr Bishop (see page 18). These tessellated patterns were most popular in Norfolk, England, while other areas favored cables, diamonds, or flags. The patterns on a basic working gansey were worked on the yoke and I have chosen to place this design on the top section of the cover to mimic this style.

Size

The cover measures approximately 8½ x 12in (21.5 x 30cm) with 2½in (6cm) for ribbed neckband

Materials

3 x 1¾oz (50g) balls damson DK yarn
Size 6 (4mm) straight needles
3 buttons, approximately
1in (2.5cm) diameter
Tapestry needle

Gauge

Not important for this project

BELOW: *The three buttons sit on a narrow band of knit 2, purl 2 rib.*

ALTERNATIVE STITCHES
Choose a pattern from another area of the country, such as the Humber star on page 23 or tree of life on page 22, and add married fishermen on page 20 at each side to make up the number of stitches to 42. Work the pattern all over the cover, if you like, and not just on the top as I have.

FRONT AND TOP HALF OF BACK

Cast on 46 sts and work 4in (10cm) st st, ending with RS facing.
Ridge:
Row 1: P.
Row 2: K.
Row 3: P.
Row 4: K.
Rep these 4 rows once more.

Next row, k2, work Row 1 of chart, k2. Continue following chart with 2 st st at each end until work measures approximately 10in (25cm) from beg, ending at the end of a 16th or 32nd row.
Repeat the 8 ridge rows.
Bind off 12 sts at beg next 2 rows and work 5in (12.5cm) in k2, p2 rib on rem sts.
Cast on 12 sts at beg next 2 rows and work in st st for 8in (20cm).
Work 3 rows k2, p2 rib.

Make three buttonholes as follows:
Work 6 sts.
* Bind off 3 sts for buttonhole.
Work 13 sts.
Repeat from * once more.
Bind off 3 sts for last buttonhole.
Work 5 sts.
Work 4 more rows rib, casting on 3 sts over those bound off on 1st of these rows.
Bind off all stitches in rib.

BOTTOM HALF OF BACK

Pick up 46 sts from cast-on row and work 4in (10cm) st st.
Work 8 rows k2, p2 rib. Bind off.

FINISHING

Fold bottom half up so that buttonhole band overlaps button band.
Sew side seams.
Sew on buttons.

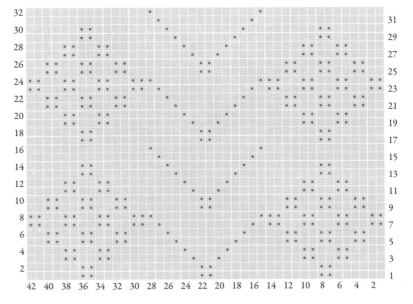

Chapter Two
TWISTED STITCHES

Once the knit and purl stitches that originated in the
late-16th century had been mastered, there was no end
to the exciting textures that could be created. In some
areas, skilled knitters took the practice a step further.
Instead of being simply knitted and purled in different
combinations, textures began to emerge featuring
stitches that had been worked out of sequence and, in
some cases, slipped altogether. The resulting fabrics
displayed repeating raised patterns of a delicate nature,
including ribbons, lattices, cables, and columns.

Twist and Slip

Influenced by the delicate embroidery of Alpine communities, twisted stitches originated in central Europe and, with a history of over 200 years, continue to play an integral role in traditional costumes of Switzerland, northern Austria and in the southern German state of Bavaria.

Originally, the most common use for twisted stitches was that of decorating socks in Germany and Austria, particularly in the Alpine regions. The decorations were known as "clocks." No-one knows precisely how this term came about, but it is thought that it could be a derivation of the word *clokke* meaning "bell," as some of the patterns could be said to resemble a bell shape.

Stitch Heritage
The designs ranged from simple columns of crossed stitches to elaborate patterns based on embroidery designs. Many of them have names that evoke the simple rural life of the communities that knitted them—honeycomb, butterfly, ribbed leaf, eye of partridge, and gullwing. Typically, such designs were placed on both sides of a sock just above the ankle. Because of the position of these designs, the crossed stitches often incorporated decreasings that would shape the ankle. Similar twisted stitch patterns were placed on the close-fitting jackets of Bavaria's regional costume, which were shaped at the waist and worn by the women with dirndl skirts. Many of them had panels of twisted stitches at each side of the front opening, and a similar, but larger motif in the center of the back. Men's socks, in particular those intended for wearing with lederhosen, were often embellished using similar techniques.

Developments Elsewhere
Some of the designs for Alpine twisted stitches are similar to those found in Celtic knotwork, with the stitches always worked through the back in order to make

LEFT: *Two women in traditional Alpine costume, rich with the embroidery that influenced many of the twisted stitches.*

them stand out. The less elaborate of these designs are similar to those found in Aran knitting (see Cable Stitches, pages 64–67) —in fact the earliest known Aran sweater is made exclusively from twisted and traveling stitches rather than the larger cables that we are familiar with today.

Similar designs to those of the Alpine socks are also found in socks from Estonia, many of which have color-patterned tops as well as twisted stitch clocks. *Krotasokkar*, knitted socks associated with the Setesdal region of Norway sometimes had twisted patterns that covered the entire leg, with the section above the ankle sometimes being made wider and more prominent. Typical stitches included cables, twists, and pleats; and while Scandinavia is particularly known for colorwork (see pages 112–115), these socks would traditionally be dyed black for men but left in their undyed white for women.

A Continental Tradition

In order to make a single twisted stitch, instead of inserting the needle from left to right through the front strand, insert it from right to left through the strand at the back, before knitting it off the needle.

On the return row, purl into the back by inserting the needle from left to right. In Continental knitting the stitches twist automatically, because the way of working —that is, by taking the yarn around the needle in a clockwise direction—causes the stitch to turn back on itself. If these stitches are then knitted into the front on the knit side, they will appear twisted. This effect can be seen to best effect in the Bavarian check stitch on page 41.

True twisted stitches cross no more than two other stitches—in fact usually only one is crossed. The effects of twisting stitches in this way can be very striking. Some examples travel across the fabric and are usually worked on a purl background, while others stay in position but stand proud of the background. Pairs of knit twisted stitches that stay in a vertical position are often worked by taking two of them together and then knitting the first stitch before slipping both stitches off the needle. This will slant the stitches to the right. For a left slant, you can knit the second stitch through the back loop then knit the first stitch through the front and slip them both off the needle. Both of these methods are used in the pattern for

the Honeycomb House Slippers on pages 42–43. The first pair of stitches is twisted to the right and the next to the left. On the following right-side row these positions are swapped over, giving a small diamond shape that resembles a honeycomb.

Stitches can also be twisted on the purl rows by purling the second stitch and then the first, before slipping them off together. This slants the stitches to the right on the right side of the piece. To slant them to the left, you simply purl two stitches together through the back loop then purl the first through the front.

Traveling twisted stitches are worked in the same way, but often on a background of purl stitches. The knit stitch passes over the top of the purl stitch that comes before it for a right slant, or the one that comes after it for a left slant. Both of these movements can be seen in the tree of life stitch on page 36. Individual stitches can be made to stand out more if they are knitted and purled into the back of the stitch on each row. You can try this with the feather stitch used in the Soft Cowl on pages 44–45. Twisted stitches of all types tend to show up best if they are worked in a smooth, light-colored wool or cotton yarn.

Twisted Stitches

Twisting stitches involves working stitches out of sequence, much in the same way that cables are made, but using two needles and not three. The result is a reasonably dense fabric, with a slightly raised texture. The stitches can be worked on knit stitches or purl stitches or a combination of both so that they slant either to the left or the right. Common twisted stitch patterns include a variety of latticework, cables, and ribs, as well as a number of popular motifs, such as butterflies and palms, the lantern and the tree of life.

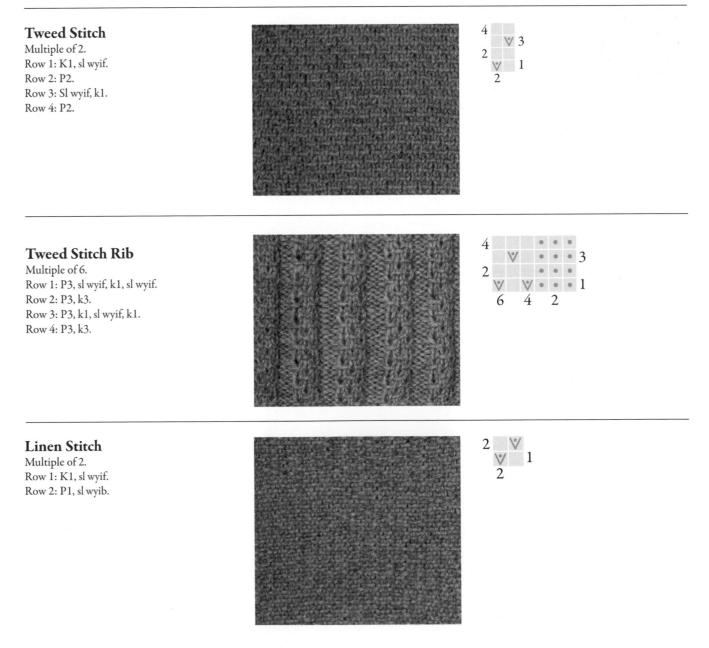

Tweed Stitch
Multiple of 2.
Row 1: K1, sl wyif.
Row 2: P2.
Row 3: Sl wyif, k1.
Row 4: P2.

Tweed Stitch Rib
Multiple of 6.
Row 1: P3, sl wyif, k1, sl wyif.
Row 2: P3, k3.
Row 3: P3, k1, sl wyif, k1.
Row 4: P3, k3.

Linen Stitch
Multiple of 2.
Row 1: K1, sl wyif.
Row 2: P1, sl wyib.

Woven Rib

Multiple of 2.
Row 1: * K1, sl wyif; repeat from * to end k1.
Row 2: P.

Woven Check

Multiple of 12.
Row 1: K9, sl3 wyif.
Row 2: P12.
Row 3: K9, sl3 wyif.
Row 4: P12.
Row 5: K9, sl3 wyif.
Row 6: P12.
Row 7: K9, sl3 wyif.
Row 8: P12.
Row 9: K9, sl3 wyif.
Row 10: P12.
Row 11: (K1, sl3 wyif) x 3.
Row 12: P12.
Row 13: (K1, sl3 wyif) x 3.
Row 14: P12.
Row 15: (K1, sl3 wyif) x 3.
Row 16: P12.

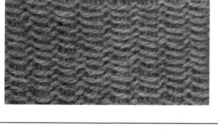

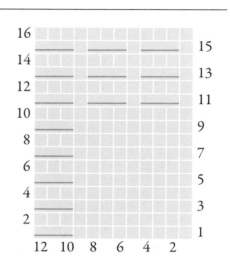

Bat Stitch

Multiple of 3.
Row 1: K.
Row 2: P1, (sl2 p-wise wyif).

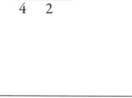

Quilting Stitch

Multiple of 6 plus 3.
hook middle = insert rn down through 5
strands and lift them onto ln, purl the 5
strands tog with next st.
Row 1: P15.
Row 2: K2, * sl5, k1. Rep from *, sl5, k2.
Row 3: P15.
Row 4: K4, insert needle under strand and
knit next st, bringing stitch out under strand,
k5. Rep from * ending last rep, k4 .
Row 5: P15.
Row 6: * K1, sl3 wyif, k1, sl5, k, sl3 wyif.
Rep from *, ending k1, sl3 wyif, k1.
Row 7: P15.
Row 8: K1, k next st under loose strand, k5.
Rep from *, to last two sts, k next st under
loose strand, k1.

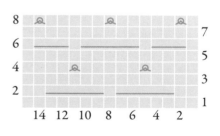

Butterfly

Multiple of 10.
hook middle = insert rn down through 5 strands and lift them onto ln, purl the 5 strands tog with next st.
Row 1: K3, sl5 wyif, k2.
Row 2: P10.
Row 3: K3, sl5 wyif, k2.
Row 4: P10.
Row 5: K3, sl5 wyif, k2.
Row 6: P10.
Row 7: K3, sl5 wyif, k2.
Row 8: P10.
Row 9: K3, sl5 wyif, k2.
Row 10: P4, hook middle, p5.

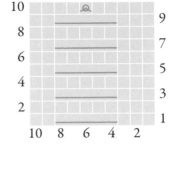

Eye of Partridge

Multiple of 2.
Row 1: K1, sl.
Row 2: P2.
Row 3: Sl, k1.
Row 4: P2.

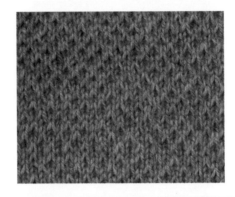

Little Cable

Multiple of 6.
Row 1: K6.
Row 2: P6.
Row 3: P1, 1/1 RC, 1/1 LC, p1.
Row 4: K1, p4, k1.
Row 5: K6.
Row 6: P6.
Row 7: K6.
Row 8: P6.
Row 9: 1/1 LC, p2, 1/1 RC.
Row 10: P6.

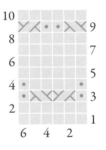

Broken Lattice

Multiple of 16.
Row 1 (WS): P16.
Row 2: * 1/1 LC, k2, 1/1 LC, 1/1 RC.
Rep from *, 1/1 LC, k2, 1/1 LC, 1/1 RC.
Row 3: P16.
Row 4: * K1, 1/1 LC, k2, 1/1 RC, k1.
Rep from *, k1, 1/1 LC, k2, 1/1 RC, k1.
Row 5: P16.
Row 6: * 1/1 RC, 1/1 LC, 1/1 RC, k2.
Rep from *, 1/1 RC, 1/1 LC, 1/1 RC, k2.
Row 7: P16.
Row 8: * K3, 1/1 LC, k2. Rep from *, 1/1 RC, k2, 1/1 LC, k3.

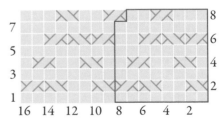

Honeycomb
Multiple of 4.
Row 1: 1/1 RC, 1/1 LC.
Row 2: P4.
Row 3: 1/1 LC, 1/1 RC.
Row 4: P4.

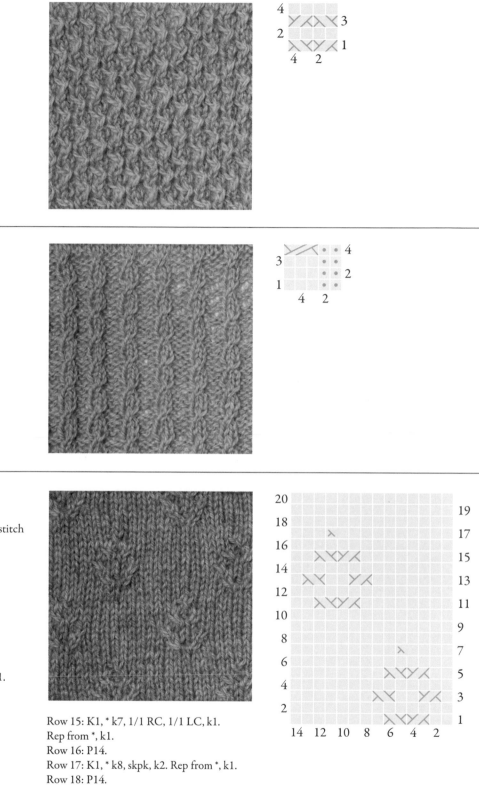

Mock Cable
Multiple of 5.
Row 1 (WS): P3, k2.
Row 2: P2, k3.
Row 3: P3, k2.
Row 4: P2, 1/2 RC.

Palms
Multiple of 12.
skpk = sl1, k1, psso, and knit again into stitch
Row 1: K1, * k1, 1/1 RC, 1/1 LC, k7.
Rep from *, k1.
Row 2: P14.
Row 3: K1, * 1/1 RC, k2, 1/1 LC, k6.
Rep from *, k1.
Row 4: P14.
Row 5: K1, * k1, 1/1 RC, 1/1 LC, k7.
Rep from *, k1.
Row 6: P14.
Row 7: K1, * k2, skpk, k8. Rep from *, k1.
Row 8: P14.
Row 9: K14.
Row 10: P14.
Row 11: K1, * k7, 1/1 RC, 1/1 LC, k1.
Rep from *, k1.
Row 12: P14.
Row 13: K1, * k6, 1/1 RC, k2, 1/1 LC.
Rep from *, k1.
Row 14: P14.

Row 15: K1, * k7, 1/1 RC, 1/1 LC, k1.
Rep from *, k1.
Row 16: P14.
Row 17: K1, * k8, skpk, k2. Rep from *, k1.
Row 18: P14.
Row 19: K14.
Row 20: P14.

"V" Panel

Multiple of 12.
Row 1 (WS): K2, p10, k2.
Row 2: P2, k3, 1/1 RC, 1/1 LC, k3, p2.
Row 3: K2, p10, k2.
Row 4: P2, k2, 1/1 RC, k2, 1/1 LC, k2, p2.
Row 5: K2, p10, k2.
Row 6: P2, k1, 1/1 RC, k4, 1/1 LC, k1, p2.
Row 7: K2, p10, k2.
Row 8: P2, 1/1 RC, k6, 1/1 LC, p2.

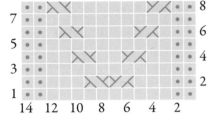

Ribbon

Multiple of 32.
Row 1: K5, 1/1 RC, k7, 1/1 RC,
1/1 LC, k7, 1/1 LC, k5.
Row 2: P7, k7, p4, k7, p7.
Row 3: K4, 1/1 RC, k7, 1/1 RC,
k2, 1/1 LC, k7, 1/1 LC, k4.
Row 4: (P6, k7) x 2, p6.
Row 5: K3, 1/1 RC, k7, 1/1 RC,
k4, 1/1 LC, k7, 1/1 LC, k3.
Row 6: P5, k7, p8, k7, p5.
Row 7: K2, 1/1 RC, k7, 1/1 RC,
k6, 1/1 LC, k7, 1/1 LC, k2.
Row 8: P4, k7, p10, k7, p4.
Row 9: K1, 1/1 RC, k7, 1/1 RC,
k8, 1/1 LC, k7, 1/1 LC, k1.
Row 10: P3, k7, p12, k7, p3.
Row 11: K2, 1/1 LC, k7, 1/1 LC,
k6, 1/1 RC, k7, 1/1 RC, k2.
Row 12: P4, k7, p10, k7, p4.
Row 13: K3, 1/1 LC, k7, 1/1 LC,
k4, 1/1 RC, k7, 1/1 RC, k3.
Row 14: P5, k7, p8, k7, p5.
Row 15: K4, 1/1 LC, k7, 1/1 LC,
k2, 1/1 RC, k7, 1/1 RC, k4.
Row 16: (P6, k7) x 2, p6.

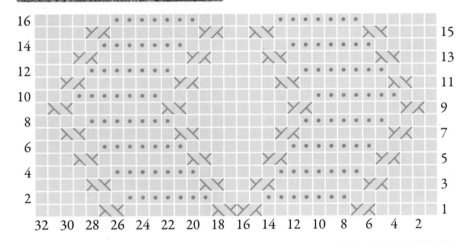

Tree of Life

Multiple of 11.
Row 1 (WS): K3, (p tbl, k1) x 2, p tbl, k3.
Row 2: P2, 1/1 RPC, p1, k tbl, p1,
1/1 LPC, p2.
Row 3: (K2, p tbl) x 3, k2.
Row 4: P1, 1/1 RPC, p2, k tbl, p2,
1/1 LPC, p1.
Row 5: K1, p tbl, k2, (p tbl) x 3, k2, p tbl, k1.
Row 6: P3, 1/1 RPC, k tbl, 1/1 LPC, p3.

Spiral Columns

Multiple of 10.
Row 1 (WS): K2, p6, * k2, p6, k2. Rep from *.
Row 2: * P2, (1/1 RC) x 3, p2. Rep from *.
Row 3: K2, p6, * k2, p6, k2. Rep from *.
Row 4: * P2, k1, (1/1 RC) x 2, k1, p2.

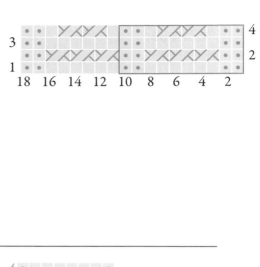

Gullwing

Multiple of 6 for the cable, and purl sts in between.
Row 1: P1, k2, (sl) x 2, k2, p1.
Row 2: K1, p2, (sl wyif) x 2, p2, k1.
Row 3: P1, 1/2 RC, 1/2 LC, p1.
Row 4: K1, p6, k1.

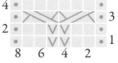

Lattice

Multiple of 9.
Row 1 (WS): P18.
Row 2: * K1, 1/1 LC, k4, 1/1 RC.
Rep from *, 1/1 LC, k4, 1/1 RC, k1.
Row 3: P18.
Row 4: * K2, 1/1 LC, k2, 1/1 RC, k1.
Rep from *, k1, 1/1 LC, k2, 1/1 RC, k2.
Row 5: P18.
Row 6: * K3, 1/1 LC, 1/1 RC, k2.
Rep from *, k2, 1/1 LC, 1/1 RC, k3.
Row 7: P18.
Row 8: * K4, 1/1 RC, k3. Rep from *,
k3, 1/1 RC, k4.
Row 9: P18.
Row 10: * K3, 1/1 RC, 1/1 LC, k2.
Rep from *, k2, 1/1 RC, 1/1 LC, k3.
Row 11: P18.
Row 12: * K2, 1/1 RC, k2, 1/1 LC, k1.

Rep from *, k1, 1/1 RC, k2, 1/1 LC, k2.
Row 13: P18.
Row 14: * K1, 1/1 RC, k4, 1/1 LC.
Rep from *, 1/1 RC, k4, 1/1 LC, k1.
Row 15: P18.
Row 16: * 1/1 RC, k6. Rep from *,
1/1 RC, k6, 1/1 RC.

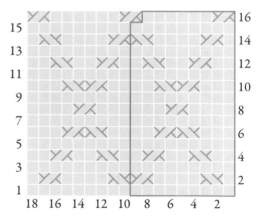

Peanut Stitch

Multiple of 10.
Row 1: P1, 1/1 RC, p7.
Row 2: K6, 1/1 LC, 1/1 RC.
Row 3: K4, p6.
Row 4: K6, p4.
Row 5: K4, p6.
Row 6: K6, 1/1 RC, 1/1 LC.
Row 7: P1, 1/1 RC, p7.
Row 8: K6, 1/1 LC, 1/1 RC.
Row 9: K4, p6.
Row 10: K6, p4.
Row 11: K4, p6.
Row 12: K6, 1/1 RC, 1/1 LC.
Row 13: P1, 1/1 RC, p7.
Row 14: K10.
Row 15: P6, 1/1 RC, p2.
Row 16: K1, 1/1 LC, 1/1 RC, k5.
Row 17: P5, k4, p1.
Row 18: K1, p4, k5.
Row 19: P5, k4, p1.
Row 20: K1, 1/1 RC, 1/1 LC, k5.
Row 21: P6, 1/1 RC, p2.

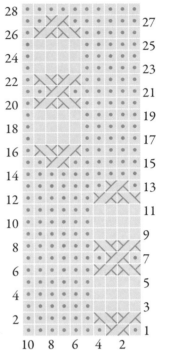

Row 22: K1, 1/1 LC, 1/1 RC, k5.
Row 23: P5, k4, p1.
Row 24: K1, p4, k5.
Row 25: P5, k4, p1.
Row 26: K1, 1/1 RC, 1/1 LC, k5.
Row 27: P6, 1/1 RC, p2.
Row 28: K10.

Zigzags

Multiple of 9.
Row 1 (WS): K8, p1, * k7, p1. Rep from *, k1.
Row 2: P1, * 1/1 LPC, p6. Rep from *, 1/1
LPC, p7.
Row 3: K7, p1, k1, * k6, p1, k1. Rep from *, k1.
Row 4: P1, * p1, 1/1 LPC, p5. Rep from *, p1,
1/1 LPC, p6.
Row 5: K6, p1, k2, * k5, p1, k2. Rep from *, k1.
Row 6: P1, * p2, 1/1 LPC, p4. Rep from *, p2,
1/1 LPC, p5.
Row 7: K5, p1, k3, * k4, p1, k3. Rep from *, k1.
Row 8: P1, * p3, 1/1 LPC, p3. Rep from *, p3,
1/1 LPC, p4.
Row 9: K4, p1, k4, * k3, p1, k4. Rep from *, k1.
Row 10: P1, * p4, 1/1 LPC, p2. Rep from *,
p4, 1/1 LPC, p3.
Row 11: K3, p1, k5, * k2, p1, k5. Rep from *, k1.
Row 12: P1, * p5, 1/1 LPC, p1. Rep from *,
p5, 1/1 LPC, p2.
Row 13: K2, p1, k6, * k1, p1, k6. Rep from *, k1.
Row 14: P1, * p6, 1/1 LPC. Rep from *, p6,
1/1 LPC, p1.
Row 15: K1, p1, k7, * p1, k7. Rep from *, k1.
Row 16: P1, * p7, k1 ; repeat from *, p7, k1, p1.
Row 17: K1, p1, k7, * p1, k7. Rep from *, k1.
Row 18: P1, * p6, 1/1 RPC. Rep from *, p6,
1/1 RPC, p1.
Row 19: K2, p1, k6, * k1, p1, k6. Rep from *, k1.
Row 20: P1, * p5, 1/1 RPC, p1. Rep from *,
p5, 1/1 RPC, p2.
Row 21: K3, p1, k5, * k2, p1, k5. Rep from *, k1.

Row 22: P1, * p4, 1/1 RPC, p2. Rep from *,
p4, 1/1 RPC, p3.
Row 23: K4, p1, k4, * k3, p1, k4. Rep from *, k1.
Row 24: P1, * p3, 1/1 RPC, p3. Rep from *,
p3, 1/1 RPC, p4.
Row 25: K5, p1, k3, * k4, p1, k3. Rep from *, k1.
Row 26: P1, * p2, 1/1 RPC, p4. Rep from *,
p2, 1/1 RPC, p5.
Row 27: K6, p1, k2, * k5, p1, k2. Rep from *, k1.
Row 28: P1, * p1, 1/1 RPC, p5. Rep from *,
p1, 1/1 RPC, p6.
Row 29: K7, p1, k1, * k6, p1, k1. Rep from *, k1.
Row 30: P1, * 1/1 RPC, p6. Rep from *, 1/1
RPC, p7.
Row 31: K8, p1, * k7, p1. Rep from *, k1.
Row 32: P1, * k1, p7. Rep from *, k1, p8.

The Lantern

Multiple of 22
Row 1 (WS): K10, p2, k10.
Row 2: P9, 1/1 RC, 1/1 LC, p9.
Row 3: K8, 1/1 LPC, p2, 1/1 RPC, k8.
Row 4: P7, 1/1 RPC, 1/1 RC, 1/1 LC, 1/1 LPC, p7.
Row 5: K6, 1/1 LPC, k1, p4, k1, 1/1 RPC, k6.
Row 6: P5, 1/1 RPC, p1, 1/1 RPC, k2, 1/1 LPC, p1, 1/1 LPC, p5.
Row 7: K4, 1/1 LPC, k2, p1, k1, p2, k1, p1, k2, 1/1 RPC, k4.
Row 8: P3, 1/1 RPC, p2, 1/1 RPC, p1, k2, p1, 1/1 LPC, p2, 1/1 LPC, p3.
Row 9: (K3, p1) x 2, k2, p2, k2, (p1, k3) x 2.
Row 10: (P2, 1/1 RPC) x 2, p2, k2, (p2, 1/1 LPC) x 2, p2.
Row 11: K2, (p1, k3) x 2, p2, (k3, p1) x 2, k2.
Row 12: P1, (1/1 RPC, p2) x 2, 1/1 RPC, (1/1 LPC, p2) x 2, 1/1 LPC, p1.
Row 13: K1, (p1, k3) x 2, p1, k2, (p1, k3) x 2, p1, k1.
Row 14: P1, (k1, p3) x 2, k1, p2, (k1, p3) x 2, k1, p1.
Row 15: K1, (p1, k3) x 2, p1, k2, (p1, k3) x 2, p1, k1.
Row 16: P1, (1/1 LPC, p2) x 2, 1/1 LPC, (1/1 RPC, p2) x 2, 1/1 RPC, p1.
Row 17: K2, (p1, k3) x 2, p2, (k3, p1) x 2, k2.
Row 18: (P2, 1/1 LPC) x 2, p2, k2, (p2, 1/1

RPC) x 2, p2.
Row 19: (K3, p1) x 2, k2, p2, k2, (p1, k3) x 2.
Row 20: P3, 1/1 LPC, p2, 1/1 LPC, p1, k2, p1, 1/1 RPC, p2, 1/1 RPC, p3.
Row 21: K4, 1/1 RPC, k2, p1, k1, p2, k1, p1, k2, 1/1 LPC, k4.
Row 22: P5, 1/1 LPC, p1, 1/1 LPC, k2, 1/1 RPC, p1, 1/1 RPC, p5.
Row 23: K6, 1/1 RPC, k1, p4, k1, 1/1 LPC, k6.
Row 24: P7, (1/1 LPC) x 2, (1/1 RPC) x 2, p7.
Row 25: K8, 1/1 RPC, p2, 1/1 LPC, k8.
Row 26: P9, 1/1 LPC, 1/1 RPC, p9.
Row 27: K10, p2, k10.
Row 28: P22.

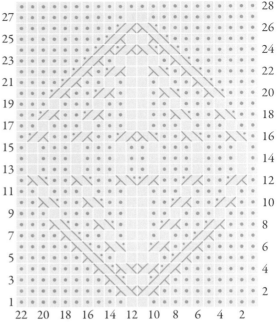

Ribbed Leaf

Multiple of 16.
Row 1 (WS): P16.
Row 2: K1, 1/1 LC, (1/1 RC) x 2, k3, (1/1 LC) x 2, 1/1 RC.
Row 3: P16.
Row 4: K2, 1/1 LC, (1/1 RC) x 2, k1, (1/1 LC) x 2, 1/1 RC, k1.
Row 5: P16.
Row 6: K1, (1/1 LC) x 2, 1/1 RC, k3, 1/1 LC, (1/1 RC) x 2.
Row 7: P16.
Row 8: K2, (1/1 LC) x 2, 1/1 RC, k1, 1/1 LC, (1/1 RC) x 2, k1.
Row 9: P16.
Row 10: K1, (1/1 LC) x 3, k3, (1/1 RC) x 3.
Row 11: P16.
Row 12: K2, (1/1 LC) x 3, k1, (1/1 RC) x 3, k1.
Row 13: P16.
Row 14: K1, (1/1 LC) x 3, k3, (1/1 RC) x 3.
Row 15: P16.
Row 16: K2, (1/1 LC) x 2, 1/1 RC, k1, 1/1 LC, (1/1 RC) x 2, k1.
Row 17: P16.
Row 18: K1, (1/1 LC) x 2, 1/1 RC, k3, 1/1 LC, (1/1 RC) x 2.
Row 19: P16.

Row 20: K2, 1/1 LC, (1/1 RC) x 2, k1, (1/1 LC) x 2, 1/1 RC, k1.
Row 21: P16.
Row 22: K1, 1/1 LC, (1/1 RC) x 2, k3, (1/1 LC) x 3.
Row 23: P16.
Row 24: K2, (1/1 RC) x 3, k1, (1/1 LC) x 3, k1.
Row 25: P16.
Row 26: K1, (1/1 RC) x 3, k3, (1/1 LC) x 3.
Row 27: P16.
Row 28: K2, (1/1 RC) x 3, k1, (1/1 LC) x 3, k1.

Twilled Stripe

Multiple of 7.
Row 1 (WS): P5, k2.
Row 2: K2, 1/1 LC, k3.
Row 3: P5, k2.
Row 4: K3, 1/1 LC, k2.
Row 5: P5, k2.
Row 6: K4, 1/1 LC, k1.
Row 7: P5, k2.
Row 8: K5, 1/1 LC.

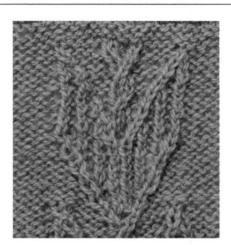

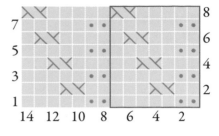

Bavarian Chevron

Multiple of 18.
Row 1 (WS): K2, p tbl, k1, p1, k3, p2, k3, p1, k1, p tbl, k2.
Row 2: P2, k tbl, (1/1 RC, p3) x 2, 1/1 LC, k tbl, p2.
Row 3: K2, (p2, k4) x 2, p2, k2.
Row 4: P2, 1/1 RC, p3, 1/1 RC, 1/1 LC, p3, 1/1 LC, p2.
Row 5: K7, p4, k7.
Row 6: P6, 1/1 RC, (k tbl) x 2, 1/1 LC, p6.
Row 7: K6, p1, k1, (p tbl) x 2, k1, p1, k6.
Row 8: P5, 1/1 RC, p1, (k tbl) x 2, p1, 1/1 LC, p5.
Row 9: K5, p2, k1, (p tbl) x 2, k1, p2, k5.
Row 10: P4, 1/1 RC, k tbl, p1, (k tbl) x 2, p1, k tbl, 1/1 LC, p4.
Row 11: K4, p1, k1, p tbl, k1, (p tbl) x 2, k1, p tbl, k1, p1, k4.
Row 12: P3, 1/1 RC, p1, k tbl, p1, (k tbl) x 2, p1, k tbl, p1, 1/1 LC, p3.
Row 13: K3, p2, k1, p tbl, k4, p tbl, k1, p2, k3.
Row 14: P2, 1/1 RC, k tbl, p1, k tbl, 1/1 RC, 1/1 LC, k tbl, p1, k tbl, 1/1 LC, p2.
Row 15: K2, p1, k1, p tbl, k1, p6, k1, p tbl, k1, p1, k2.
Row 16: P2, (k tbl, p1) x 2, 1/1 RC, k2, 1/1 LC, (p1, k tbl) x 2, p2.

Row 17: K2, (p tbl, k1) x 2, p1, k1, p2, k1, p1, (k1, p tbl) x 2, k2.
Row 18: P2, k tbl, p1, k tbl, (1/1 RC, p1) x 2, 1/1 LC, k tbl, p1, k tbl, p2.
Row 19: K2, p tbl, k1, (p2, k2) x 2, p2, k1, p tbl, k2.
Row 20: P2, k tbl, p1, 1/1 RC, p2, k2, p2, 1/1 LC, p1, k1, p2.

Bavarian Check

Multiple of 28

Row 1: (P1, 1/1 RC) x 3, p1, (k tbl) x 8.
Row 2: (P tbl) x 8, (k1, p2) x 3, k1.
Row 3: (P1, 1/1 RC) x 3, p1, (k tbl) x 8.
Row 4: (P tbl) x 8, (k1, p2) x 3, k1.
Row 5: (P1, 1/1 RC) x 3, p1, (k tbl) x 8.
Row 6: (P tbl) x 8, (k1, p2) x 3, k1.
Row 7: (P1, 1/1 RC) x 3, p1, (k tbl) x 8.
Row 8: (P tbl] x 8, (k1, p2) x 3, k1.
Row 9: (P1, 1/1 RC) x 3, p1, (k tbl) x 8.
Row 10: (P tbl) x 8, k1, p8, k1.
Row 11: P1, (k tbl) x 8, p1, (1/1 RC, k1) x 2, 1/1 RC.
Row 12: P8, k1, (p tbl) x 8, k1.
Row 13: P1, (k tbl) x 8, p1, (1/1 RC, k1) x 2, 1/1 RC.
Row 14: P8, k1, (p tbl) x 8, k1.
Row 15: P1, (k tbl) x 8, p1, (1/1 RC, k1) x 2, 1/1 RC.

Row 16: P8, k1, (p tbl) x 8, k1.
Row 17: P1, (k tbl) x 8, p1, (1/1 RC, k1) x 2, 1/1 RC.
Row 18: P8, k1, (p tbl) x 8, k1.
Row 19: P1, (k tbl) x 8, p1, (1/1 RC, k1) x 2, 1/1 RC.
Row 20: P8, k1, (p tbl) x 8, k1.

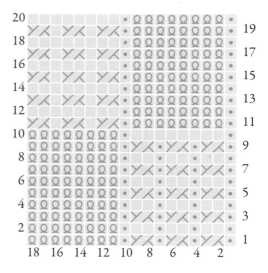

Bavarian Clock

Multiple of 18.

Round 1: P1, k tbl, p4, (k tbl) x 2, p2, (k tbl) x 2, p4, k tbl, p1.
Round 2: P1, k tbl, p4, 1/1 LC, p2, 1/1 LC, p4, k tbl, p1.
Round 3: P1, k tbl, p3, (1/1 RPC, 1/1 LPC) x 2, p3, k tbl, p1.
Round 4: P1, k tbl, p3, k tbl, p2, 1/1 LC, p2, k tbl, p3, k tbl, p1.
Round 5: P1, k tbl, p3, (1/1 LPC, 1/1 RPC) x 2, p3, k tbl, p1.
Round 6: P1, k tbl, p4, 1/1 LC, p2, 1/1 LC, p4, k tbl, p1.
Round 7: P1, k tbl, p3, (1/1 RPC, 1/1 LPC) x 2, p3, k tbl, p1.
Round 8: P1, k tbl, p3, k tbl, p2, 1/1 LC, p2, k tbl, p3, k tbl, p1.
Round 9: P1, k tbl, p3, (1/1 LPC, 1/1 RPC) x 2, p3, k tbl, p1.
Round 10: P1, k tbl, p4, 1/1 LC, p2, 1/1 LC, p4, k tbl, p1.
Round 11: P1, k tbl, p3, (1/1 RPC, 1/1 LPC) x 2, p3, k tbl, p1.
Round 12: P1, k tbl, p3, k tbl, p2, 1/1 LC, p2, k tbl, p3, k tbl, p1.
Round 13: P1, k tbl, p3, k tbl, p2, (k tbl) x 2, p2, k tbl, p3, k tbl, p1.
Round 14: P1, k tbl, p3, k tbl, p2, 1/1 LC, p2, k tbl, p3, k tbl, p1.

Round 15: P1, k tbl, p3, k tbl, p2, (k tbl) x 2, p2, k tbl, p3, k tbl, p1.
Round 16: P1, k tbl, p3, k tbl, p2, 1/1 LC, p2, k tbl, p3, k tbl, p1.
Round 17: P1, k tbl, p3, k tbl, p2, (k tbl) x 2, p2, k tbl, p3, k tbl, p1.
Round 18: P1, k tbl, p3, k tbl, p2, 1/1 LC, p2, k tbl, p3, k tbl, p1.
Round 19: P1, k tbl, p3, k tbl, p2, (k tbl) x 2, p2, k tbl, p3, k tbl, p1.
Round 20: P1, k tbl, p3, k tbl, p2, 1/1 LC, p2, k tbl, p3, k tbl, p1.

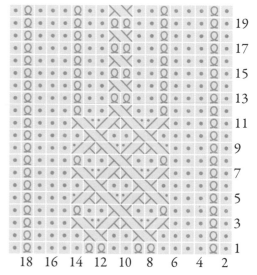

Honeycomb House Slippers

Honeycomb patterns are often used as filler stitches in Aran knitting. Sometimes they can be seen as wide central panels and at other times they are used to make the sides of a garment. This pattern results in a firm and warm fabric, ideal for a pair of cozy house slippers. The firm fabric will help them to keep their shape.

Size
Ladies small (medium, large)

Materials
2 x 1¾oz (50g) balls light-pink DK yarn
Size 7 (4.5mm) straight needles
Size 7 (4.5mm) 24in (60cm) or longer circular needle (or dpns)
10ft (3m) ribbon
Tapestry needle

Gauge
26 sts and 28 rows = 4in (10cm) over g st

HONEYCOMB PATTERN
Row 1: *1/1 RC, 1/1 LC. Rep from *.
Row 2: P.
Row 3: *1/1 LC, 1/1 RC. Rep from *.
Row 4: P..

SOLE
Cast on 12 (16, 16) sts and knit 4 rows.
Inc at each end of next row and follow 4th row to 16 (18, 18) sts.
Knit to 8 (9, 10in) (20, 23, 25cm)
Bind off all sts but last one; don't break yarn.

UPPER
Cast on 8 (8, 12) sts, incl st on needle.
Using circular needle, knit these 8 (10, 10) sts then pick up and knit 42 (46, 50) sts along side of sole, knit 12 (16, 16) sts from cast-on edge, pick up and knit 42 (46, 50) sts along other side of sole, cast on 8 (8, 12) sts.
Knit 4 rows working back and forth, not in the round.

Row 1: K8 (8, 12), p to last 8 (8, 12), k8 (8, 12).
Keeping these edge sts in garter stitch, work honeycomb pattern for 8 rows.
Row 9: K8 (8, 12), p40, (44, 48), p2tog, p12 (16, 16), p2tog tbl, p40 (44, 48), k8 (8, 12).
Row 10: K47 (51, 59), k2tog, pattern 12, ssk, k to end.
Row 11: Sl1, p 12 (12, 16) turn.
Row 12: Sl1, pattern 12, ssk, turn.
Rep from * ending these 2 rows until there are 41 (45, 54) sts left at each end.
Knit to end.
Next row: (P1, yf, p2tog) to end.
Next row: K.
Bind off.

FINISHING
Join back seam and sew to end of sole.
Thread ribbon through holes, starting and ending at center back seam.

ALTERNATIVE STITCHES
If you would like to use a different stitch then choose a small one that is a multiple of two or four stitches—perhaps linen stitch on page 32 or woven rib on page 33. The wider stitches would probably not be suitable, because they would be cut into when you work the decreases around the top of the foot.

LEFT: *The honeycomb stitch gives these slippers their dense, cozy texture.*

Soft Cowl

Twisted stitches like the one used here have long been popular in the Alpine regions of Europe. They are most familiar on socks and mittens but I thought it would be interesting to try one out on something larger. I chose the twisted feather stitch, because it does not have a definite beginning and end. The stitch has the added bonus of looking good from both sides, which is an important consideration when making a scarf or moebius twisted cowl.

Size
The cowl measures approximately
7 x 50in (18 x 126cm)

Materials
3 x 1¾oz (50g) balls purple sport-weight yarn
Size 3 (3.25mm) straight needles
Tapestry needle

Gauge
Not important for this project

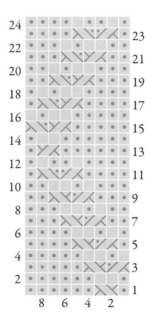

TWISTED FEATHER STITCH
Row 1: P1, 1/1 LC, p6.
Row 2: K6, p2, k1.
Row 3: 1/1 RPC, 1/1 LC, p5.
Row 4: K5, p2, k1, p1.
Row 5: P1, 1/1 RPC, 1/1 LC, p4.
Row 6: K4, p2, k1, p1, k1.
Row 7: P2, 1/1 RPC, 1/1 LC, p3.
Row 8: K3, p2, k1, p1, k2.
Row 9: P3, 1/1 RPC, 1/1 LC, p2.
Row 10: K2, p2, k1, p1, k3.
Row 11: P4, 1/1 RPC, 1/1 LPC, p1.
Row 12: K1, p1, k2, p1, k4.
Row 13: P6, 1/1 RC, p1.
Row 14: K1, p2, k6.
Row 15: P5, 1/1 RC, 1/1 LPC.
Row 16: P1, k1, p2, k5.
Row 17: P4, 1/1 RC, 1/1 LPC, p1.
Row 18: K1, p1, k1, p2, k4.
Row 19: P3, 1/1 RC, 1/1 LPC, p2.
Row 20: K2, p1, k1, p2, k3.
Row 21: P2, 1/1 RC, 1/1 LPC, p3.
Row 22: K3, p1, k1, p2, k2.
Row 23: P1, 1/1 RPC, 1/1 LPC, p4.
Row 24: K4, p1, k2, p1, k1.

Loosely cast on 42 sts and knit 2 rows.
Work from chart or pattern instructions, repeating them 4 times across the row and keeping 3 sts in moss stitch at beg and end of every row.
Continue until piece measures approximately 50in (126cm) ending on a row 24.
Knit 2 rows.
Bind off loosely.

FINISHING
Either join cast-on and bind-off edges with right sides facing, or give cowl one twist and join with one wrong side and one right side facing to form a moebius cowl.

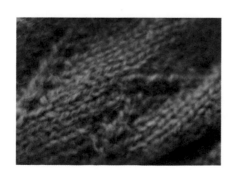

RIGHT: *The twisted feather stitch gives this cowl its soft, lightly textured surface.*

ALTERNATIVE STITCHES
Bear in mind that if you are going to substitute this stitch with one of the others from this section, you should choose one that is easily reversible. The zigzag pattern shown on page 38 would be suitable, and would show up as purl stitches on a knit stitch background.

Chapter Three
RAISED STITCHES

Bobbles, knots, buds, and loops are among the various
knitting techniques that have developed in almost
all traditions, for creating a deeper or more intricate
texture in a finished piece. Achieved by increasing and
decreasing stitches in a number of ways, they can be
most effective when used as accents or repeated motifs.
Raised stitches are not just about decoration, however.
Thick-stitched leaf patterns for babies' blankets and
the bobbles on an Aran sweater or a knitted beret are
as much about creating warmth as a decorative finish.

Increase, Decrease

Almost all knitting traditions include raised stitches of one kind or another—from the delicate traveling stitches of Alpine twists to chunky Aran cables and plaits. Among them can be found numerous fun knots and bobbles as well as a wide range of embossed leaves, buds, and flowers.

Raised stitches encompass many different techniques, all of them used for giving a thicker and more textured surface to a piece of knitting.

Bobble Traditions

Perhaps the most familiar application of the bobble can be seen within the cable patterns on Aran sweaters. Here you might see diamonds with bobbles at their centers or diamonds with pairs or quartets of bobbles between them. There is also a chevron and bobble design and a framed bobble design. This last resembles the medallion moss swatch on page 71, but with a bobble at its center. There are also latticework patterns that sometimes have bobbles at their crossing points. In some Arans and garments from the Tyrol, in northern Austria, the bobbles are arranged in groups, as in the nosegay stitch on page 56, in order to form flowers. In Tyrolean knitting, these would then traditionally be embellished with colorful embroidery.

To make a basic five-stitch bobble, a knit stitch is then purled, knitted, purled, and knitted into. The work is turned and the stitches knitted or purled again, depending on whether a smooth (knitted) or nobbly (purled) texture is sought after on the right side. The work is turned again and all the stitches either knitted or purled once more. Finally, the same stitches are worked one last time, then the second, third, fourth, and fifth stitches lifted one at a time, over the first stitch. This decreases the stitches on the needle to the original count, and a bobble appears on the right side of the work. The bobbles used in the Raspberry Beret on pages 58–59 are made by working knit and purl stitches into the same stitch, but you can use whichever method you prefer.

ABOVE: *The fashion for "white knitting" that had begun in the drawing rooms of British and American homes during the Victorian era continued well into the 20th century. This photograph of an elderly woman in her richly textured shawl was taken in 1919.*

Smaller bobbles are made in the same way, by increasing to three stitches, or by increasing and decreasing on the same row. This is the method used to create the "nupps" seen in Estonian lace knitting. You can increase as many times as you want into one stitch, depending on how large you want your nupp to be, and then, on the next row, knit or purl all the increased stitches together.

The lily of the valley pattern on page 57 is typical of the stitches combined with eyelets as used in Estonian knitting, where lace shawls became fashionable during the late-19th century, when wealthy women would travel to the mud baths of Haapsalu. The local women imitated the fashionable lace shawls that these visitors wore, adding their own interpretations to make them unique to the region. They devised ways of making these light and lacy shawls a little more substantial by

LEFT: *Lace leaves have been worked on a reverse stockinette stitch background in order to achieve an embossed look for the main design.*

In traditional patterns, a leaf might "grow" from a knitted stem or it would be made out of one stitch by working a yarn over at each side of a central stitch. An interesting pattern can be made by working two leaves forming a "V" shape and then working a group of bobbles above them in the shape of a flower, as in the flower stitch on page 53, but with more bobbles.

All leaf patterns are made by increasing, either with yarn overs to form a vertical row of holes or working another form of increase such as a lifted or invisible increase, which doesn't leave holes. These increased stitches then need to be decreased back to one over a number of rows. How often you decrease determines the shape of the leaves; frequent increases will make it short and squat, while spaced increases will produce a longer, narrower leaf.

Looped Knitting

Another form of raised stitch is that of looped knitting. Again, there are a number of different methods, depending on how thick you want the finished fabric, or how long you want the loops. The traditional way is to wrap the yarn three times around the finger on alternate stitches and on every wrong-side row. You then knit the stitch again after making the loops. You can cut through these stitches without them becoming unraveled. The more times you wrap the yarn around your finger, the thicker the finished fabric will be. The same applies to how frequently you make each loop, too. If you work it in every stitch on every wrong side row it will be thicker than if you do it less frequently.

This is a similar technique to that used among logging communities of North East America and Canada for making thick, "buff" mittens with loops on the inside. Because the stitch is knitted twice it doesn't unravel when it is cut and eventually felts, through use, into a dense and almost waterproof fabric. This felting only occurs with wool, however, and will not work with acrylic fiber.

adding bobbles, or "nupps" to increase their weight. An increased weight meant that the knitters would get a better price for their work. They became extremely desirable and are still being made and sold to tourists today.

Traditional Leaf Patterns

Raised leaf patterns often featured on the counterpanes and blankets that became very popular in Britain and the United States during the Victorian era, although they had been in use throughout Europe before that. During the 18th century, cotton began to be imported into Europe from the East and this spawned the craze for "white knitting." Home-grown cotton was already available in the United States, where enthusiasts were quick to take up this technique. Blankets and counterpanes were usually made up of squares, knitted in cotton, which could be bleached to a pure white, unlike wool. This fabric looked fresh and could be laundered more easily than wool. The squares were joined together in blocks of four before an edging or border was added, often also incorporating some raised leaf or bobble pattern.

Although the generic leaf design is now known as English Garden, it was most popular in France, outlined with bands of different lace and textured patterns instead of the rows of eyelets that were more commonly used in England. Favorite English designs were often based on the foxglove pattern on page 54, again with bands of reverse stockinette stitch, or rows of eyelets between them. After all the squares had been sewn together, a border with similar designs would be knitted and sewn on.

Raised Stitches

Knitting raised stitches involves many different techniques, all of them used for giving a more textured surface to the knitting. Some of them are akin to textured stitches (see pages 14–23) and some to cables (see pages 68–79). Some are made by increasing and decreasing stitches over a number of rows, as in the leaf motifs, and others make several stitches out of one, which are then decreased back to one again on the same or following row, as with the bobble and knot stitches.

Diamond Drops
Multiple of 4.
pop = yrn, p2, pass made st over 2 p sts.
Row 1: K1, pop, k2.
Row 2: P4.
Row 3: K3, pop.
Row 4: P4.

Tiny Towers
Multiple of 8 plus 1.
Row 1: P1, * yo, p2tog, p6. Rep from *.
Row 2: * K7, p1. Rep from *, k1.
Row 3: P1, * k1, p7. Rep from *.
Row 4: * K7, p1. Rep from *, k1.
Row 5: P1, * k1, p7. Rep from *.
Row 6: * K7, p1. Rep from *, k1.
Row 7: P1, * k1, p7. Rep from *.
Row 8: P9.
Row 9: P1, * p4, yo, p2tog, p2. Rep from *.
Row 10: * K3, p1, k4. Rep from *, k1.
Row 11: P1, * p4, k1, p3. Rep from *.
Row 12: * K3, p1, k4. Rep from *, k1.
Row 13: P1, * p4, k1, p3. Rep from *.
Row 14: * K3, p1, k4. Rep from *, k1.
Row 15: P1, * p4, k1, p3. Rep from *.
Row 16: P9.

Spaced Knots

Multiple of 6 plus 5.
Repeat sts in parentheses.
incto4 = k1, p1, k1, p1, all into next stitch.
s3kpo = sl3, k1, pass 3 sl sts over.
Row 1: K.
Row 2: P.
Row 3 : K.
Row 4 : P.
Row 5 : * K5, incto4. Rep from *, k5.
Row 6 : P5, * s3kpo, p5. Rep from *.
Row 7: K.
Row 8: P.
Row 9: K.
Row 10: P.
Row 11: * K2, incto4, k3. Rep from *,
k2, incto4, k2.

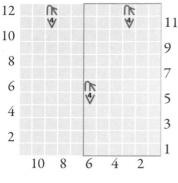

Row 12: P2, s3kpo, p2, * p3, s3kpo, p2.
Rep from *.

Bud Stitch

Multiple of 7.
Row 1: P5, * k1, yo, p5. Rep from *.
Row 2: K5, * p2, k5. Rep from *.
Row 3: P5, * k2, p5. Rep from *.
Row 4: K5, * p2, k5. Rep from *.
Row 5: P5, * k2, p5. Rep from *.
Row 6: K5, p2tog, k5.
Row 7: P2, * k1, yo, p5. Rep from *, k1, yo, p2.
Row 8: K2, p2, k2, * k3, p2, k2. Rep from *.
Row 9: P2, * k2, p5. Rep from *, k2, p2.
Row 10: K2, p2, k2, * k3, p2, k2. Rep from *.
Row 11: * P2, k2, p3. Rep from *, p2, k2, p2.
Row 12: K2, p2tog, k3, * k2, p2tog, k2.
Rep from *.

Tulips

Multiple of 13.
incto6 = (p1, k1) 3 times in same stitch.
Row 1: P13.
Row 2: K13.
Row 3: P8, incto6, p9.
Row 4: K6, p6, k6.
Row 5: P6, k6, p6.
Row 6: K6, p6, k6.
Row 7: K2tog, p2tog, p2, (k2, yo) x 2, k2, p2, (p2tog) x 2.
Row 8: K4, p8, k4.
Row 9: (P2tog) x 2, (k2tog, yo, k1, yo) x 2, k2tog, (p2tog) x 2.
Row 10: K2, p9, k2.

Bobbles

Multiple of 10 plus 5.
Row 1: K.
Row 2: P.
Row 3: K.
Row 4: P.
Row 5: * K7, bobble, k2. Rep from *, k5.
Row 6: P.
Row 7: K.
Row 8: P.
Row 9: K.
Row 10: P.
Row 11: * K2, bobble, k7. Rep from *, k2, bobble, k2.
Row 12: P.

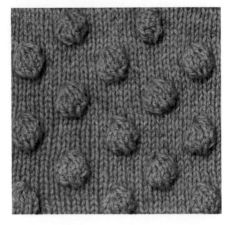

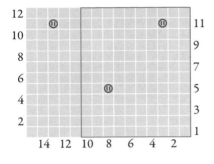

Flower Buds

Multiple of 10.
Small bobble = incto5 then pass each st one at a time over 5th st.
Row 1: K10.
Row 2: P10.
Row 3: K10.
Row 4: P10.
Row 5: K2, yo, ssk, k6.
Row 6: P10.
Row 7: K2tog, yo, k1, yo, ssk, k5.
Row 8: P10.
Row 9: K2, small bobble, k7.
Row 10: P10.
Row 11: K10.
Row 12: P10.
Row 13: K10.
Row 14: P10.

Row 15: K7, yo, ssk, k1.
Row 16: P10.
Row 17: K5, k2tog, yo, k1, yo, ssk.
Row 18: P10.
Row 19: K7, bobble, k2.
Row 20: P10.

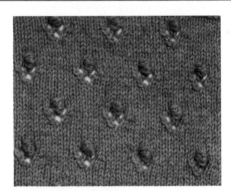

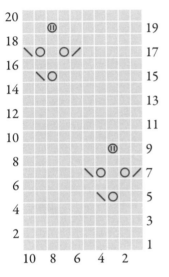

Diamond Bobble

Multiple of 12.
Bobble: (k, p, k) into next st, turn, k3, turn, p3, turn, k3; s1, k2tog, psso.
Row 1: * P1, (k3, bobble) x 2, k3. Rep from *, p1.
Row 2: P13.
Row 3: * K1, p1, k9, p1. Rep from *, k1.
Row 4: P13.
Row 5: * K2, p1, k3, bobble, k3, p1, k1. Rep from *, k1.
Row 6: P13.
Row 7: * K3, p1, k5, p1, k2. Rep from *, k1.
Row 8: P13.
Row 9: * Bobble, (k3, p1) x 2, k3. Rep from *, bobble.
Row 10: P13.
Row 11: * K5, p1, k1, p1, k4. Rep from *, k1.
Row 12: P13.
Row 13: * K2, bobble, k3, p1, k3, bobble, k1. Rep from *, k1.
Row 14: P13.
Row 15: * K5, p1, k1, p1, k4. Rep from *, k1.
Row 16: P13.
Row 17: * Bobble, (k3, p1) x 2, k3.

Rep from *, bobble.
Row 18: P13.
Row 19: * K3, p1, k5, p1, k2. Rep from *, k1.
Row 20: P13.
Row 21: * K2, p1, k3, bobble, k3, p1, k1. Rep from *, k1.
Row 22: P13.
Row 23: * K1, p1, k9, p1. Rep from *, k1.
Row 24: P13.

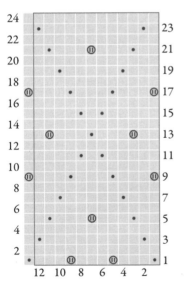

Stem and Buds

Multiple of 13.
Bobble = (k1, p1, k1, p1) all into next st, k5tog tbl.
Row 1 (WS): K6, p1, k6.
Row 2: P5, 1/1 RC, p6.
Row 3: K6, p2, k5.
Row 4: P4, 1/1 RC, k1, p6.
Row 5: K6, p1, k1, p1, k4.
Row 6: P3, 1/1 RC, p1, k1, p6.
Row 7: K6, p1, k2, p1, k3.
Row 8: P2, 1/1 RC, p2, k1, p6.
Row 9: K6, p1, k3, p1, k2.
Row 10: P2, bobble, p3, k1, p6.
Row 11: K5, 1/1 LC, k6.
Row 12: P6, k2, p5.
Row 13: K4, 1/1 LC, p1, k6.
Row 14: P6, k1, p1, k1, p4.
Row 15: K3, 1/1 LC, k1, p1, k6.
Row 16: P6, k1, p2, k1, p3.

Row 17: K2, 1/1 LC, k2, p1, k6.
Row 18: P6, k1, p3, k1, p2.
Row 19: K1, 1/1 LC, k3, p1, k6.
Row 20: P6, k1, p4, bobble, p1.

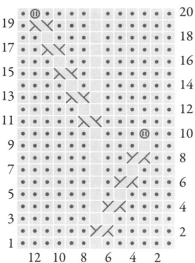

Flowers

Multiple of 17.
Row 1: * P7, 1/2 RC, p4. Rep from *, p3.
Row 2: K3, * k4, p3, k7. Rep from *.
Row 3: * P8, M1, yo, k1, yo, M1, p5.
Rep from *, p3.
Row 4: K3, * k4, p7, k7. Rep from *.
Row 5: P6, k2tog, k2, yo, k tbl, yo, k2, ssk, p3. Rep from *, p3.
Row 6: K3, * k3, p3, k1, p tbl, k1, p3, k6.
Rep from *.
Row 7: * P5, k2tog, k2, yo, p1, k tbl, p1, yo, k2, ssk, p2. Rep from *, p3.
Row 8: K3, * k2, p3, k2, p tbl, k2, p3, k5.
Rep from *.
Row 9: * P4, k2tog, k2, yo, p2, k tbl, p2, yo, k2, ssk, p1. Rep from *, p3.
Row 10: K3, * k1, p3, k3, p tbl, k3, p3, k4.
Rep from *.
Row 11: * P3, (k2tog) x 2, yo, p3, k tbl, p3, yo, (ssk) x 2. Rep from *, p3.
Row 12: K3, * p2, k4, p tbl, k4, p2, k3.
Rep from *.
Row 13: * P3, k2tog, p4, bobble, p4, ssk.
Rep from *, p3.
Row 14: K17.
Row 15: * 1/2 RC, p11. Rep from *, 1/2 RC.
Row 16: P3, * k11, p3. Rep from *.
Row 17: * K2, yo, M1, p13, M1. Rep from *, yo, k1, p1.
Row 18: K1, p2, * p2, k11, p4, k1. Rep from *.
Row 19: * P1, k tbl, yo, k2, ssk, p10, k2.
Rep from *, yo, k tbl, p1.

Row 20: K1, p tbl, k1, * p3, k9, p4, p tbl, k1.
Rep from *.
Row 21: * P1, k tbl, p1, yo, k2, ssk, p8, k2, yo.
Rep from *, p1, k tbl, p1.
Row 22: K1, p tbl, k1, * k1, p3, k7, p3, k2, p tbl, k1. Rep from *.
Row 23: * P1, k tbl, p2, yo, k2, p7, k2, yo, p1.
Rep from *, p1, k bl, p1.
Row 24: K1, p tbl, k1, * k2, p3, k5, p3, k3, p tbl, k1. Rep from *.
Row 25: * P1, k tbl, p3, yo, (ssk) x 2, p3, (k2tog) x 2, yo, p2. Rep from *, p1, k tbl, p1.
Row 26: K1, p tbl, k1, * (k3, p2) x 2, k4, p tbl, k1. Rep from *.
Row 27: * P1, bobble, p4, ssk, p3, k2tog, p3.
Rep from *, p1, bobble, p1.
Row 28: K17.

Alternate Bobble Stripe

Multiple of 10.

Bobble = (k1, p1, k1, p1, k1) into stitch, turn, k5, turn, k5tog.

Row 1: P2, k1, p4, k1, p2.
Row 2: K2, p1, k4, p1, k2.
Row 3: P2, bobble, p4, k1, p2.
Row 4: K2, p1, k4, p1, k2.
Row 5: P2, k1, p4, k1, p2.
Row 6: K2, p1, k4, p1, k2.
Row 7: P2, bobble, p4, k1, p2.
Row 8: K2, p1, k4, p1, k2.
Row 9: P2, k1, p4, k1, p2.
Row 10: K2, p1, k4, p1, k2.
Row 11: P2, bobble, p4, k1, p2.
Row 12: K2, p1, k4, p1, k2.
Row 13: P2, k1, p4, k1, p2.
Row 14: K2, p1, k4, p1, k2.
Row 15: P2, bobble, p4, k1, p2.
Row 16: K2, p1, k4, p1, k2.
Row 17: P2, k1, p4, k1, p2.
Row 18: K2, p1, k4, p1, k2.
Row 19: P2, bobble, p4, k1, p2.
Row 20: K2, p1, k4, p1, k2.
Row 21: P2, k1, p4, k1, p2.
Row 22: K2, bobble, k4, p1, k2.
Row 23: P2, k1, p4, k1, p2.
Row 24: K2, p1, k4, p1, k2.
Row 25: P2, k1, p4, k1, p2.
Row 26: K2, bobble, k4, p1, k2.

Row 27: P2, k1, p4, k1, p2.
Row 28: K2, p1, k4, p1, k2.
Row 29: P2, k1, p4, k1, p2.
Row 30: K2, bobble, k4, p1, k2.
Row 31: P2, k1, p4, k1, p2.
Row 32: K2, p1, k4, p1, k2.
Row 33: P2, k1, p4, k1, p2.
Row 34: K2, bobble, k4, p1, k2.
Row 35: P2, k1, p4, k1, p2.
Row 36: K2, p1, k4, p1, k2.
Row 37: P2, k1, p4, k1, p2.
Row 38: K2, bobble, k4, p1, k2.
Row 39: P2, k1, p4, k1, p2.
Row 40: K2, p1, k4, p1, k2.

Foxgloves

Multiple of 8 plus 4.

Row 1: P3.
Row 2: K3.
Row 3: P3, cast on 10.
Row 4: P10, k3.
Row 5: P3, ssk, k6, k2tog.
Row 6: P8, k3.
Row 7: P3, ssk, k4, k2tog.
Row 8: P6, k3.
Row 9: P3, ssk, k2, k2tog.
Row 10: P4, k3.
Row 11: P3, ssk, k2tog.
Row 12: P2, k3.
Row 13: P3, k2tog.
Row 14: P1, k3.
Row 15: P2, p2tog.
Row 16: K3.

Bramble Stitch

Multiple of 4.

Row 1: P1 * p4. Rep from *.
Row 2: * (P1, k1, p1) in 1 st, k3tog.
Rep from *, k1.
Row 3: P1 * p4. Rep from *.
Row 4: * k3tog, (p1, k1, p1) in 1 st.
Rep from *, k1.

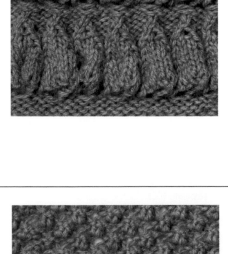

Embossed Leaf

Multiple of 12.
Row 1: * P5, yo, k1, yo, p5. Rep from *.
Row 2: * K5, p3, k5. Rep from *.
Row 3: * P5, (k1, yo) x 2, k1, p5. Rep from *.
Row 4: * K5, p5, k5. Rep from *.
Row 5: * P5, k2, yo, k1, yo, k2, p5. Rep from *.
Row 6: * K5, p7, k5. Rep from *.
Row 7: * P5, k3, yo, k1, yo, k3, p5. Rep from *.
Row 8: * K5, p9, k5. Rep from *.
Row 9: * P5, k3, sk2p, k3, p5. Rep from *.
Row 10: * K5, p7, k5. Rep from *.
Row 11: * P5, k2, sk2p, k2, p5. Rep from *.
Row 12: * K5, p5, k5. Rep from *.
Row 13: * P5, k1, sk2p, k1, p5. Rep from *.
Row 14: * K5, p3, k5. Rep from *.
Row 15: * P5, sk2p, p5. Rep from *.
Row 16: * K5, p1, k5. Rep from *.
Row 17: P.
Row 18: K.

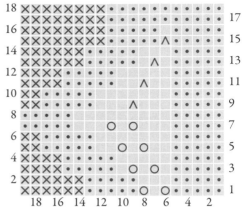

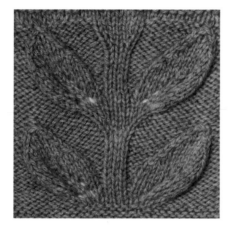

Embossed Double Leaf

Row 1 (WS): K10, p9, k10.
Row 2: P8, p2tog, (K1, yo) x 2, kfb, k2, kfb, (k1, yo) x 2, k1, p2tog, p8.
Row 3: K9, p5, k1, p3, k1, p5, k9.
Row 4: P7, p2tog, k2, yo, k1, yo, k2, pfb, k3, pfb, k2, yo, k1, yo, k2, p2tog, p7.
Row 5: K8, p7, k2, p3, k2, p7, k8.
Row 6: P6, p2tog, k3, yo, k1, yo, k3, pfb, p1, k3, p1, pfb, k3, yo, k1, yo, k3, p2tog, p6.
Row 7: K7, p9, k3, p3, k3, p9, k7.
Row 8: P5, p2tog, k4, yo, k1, yo, k4, pfb, p2, k3, p2, pfb, k4, yo, k1, yo, k4, p2tog, p5.
Row 9: K6, p11, k4, p3, k4, p11, k6.
Row 10: P4, p2tog, ssk, k7, k2tog, pfb, p3, k3, p3, pfb, ssk, k7, k2tog, p2tog, p4.

Row 11: K5, p9, k5, p3, k5, p9, k5.
Row 12: P3, p2tog, ssk, k5, k2tog, pfb, p4, k3, p4, pfb, ssk, k5, k2tog, p2tog, p3.
Row 13: K4, p7, k6, p3, k6, p7, k4.
Row 14: P2, p2tog, ssk, k3, k2tog, pfb, p5, (k1, m1) x 2, k1, p5, pfb, ssk, k3, k2tog, p2tog, p2.
Row 15: K3, (p5, k7) x 2, p5, k3.
Row 16: P1, p2tog, ssk, k1, k2tog, pfb, p6, k1, m1, k3, m1, k1, p6, pfb, ssk, k1, k2tog, p2tog, p1.
Row 17: K2, p3, k8, p7, k8, p3, k2.
Row 18: P2, sk2p, p6, p2tog, k1, m1, k5, m1, k1, p2tog, p6, sk2p, p2.

Carillon

Multiple of 12.

incto5 = (k1, p1, k1, p1, k1) all into next st.

Row 1 (WS): K2, incto5, (k2, p tbl) x 3, k2, incto5, k2.

Row 2: P2, k5, (p2, k tbl) x 3, p2, k5, p2.

Row 3: K2, p5, (k2, p tbl) x 3, k2, p5, k2.

Row 4: P2, dec 3, (p2, k tbl) x 3, p2, dec 3, p2.

Row 5: K2, p3, k2, p tbl, p2, p tbl, p1, k1, p tbl, k2, P3, k2.

Row 6: P2, sl1, k2tog, psso, (p2, k tbl) x 3, p2, sl1, k2tog, psso, p2.

Row 7: (K2, p tbl, k2, incto5) x 2, k2, p tbl, k2.

Row 8: (P2, k tbl, p2, k5) x 2, p2, k tbl, p2.

Row 9: (K2, p tbl, k2, P5) x 2, k2, p tbl, k2.

Row 10: (P2, k tbl, p2, dec 3) x 2, p2, k tbl, p2.

Row 11: (K2, p tbl, k2, p3) x 2, k2, p tbl, k2.

Row 12: (P2, k tbl, p2, sl1, k2tog, psso) x 2, p2, k tbl, p2.

Row 13: (K2, p tbl) x 2, k2, incto5, (k2, p tbl) x 2, k2.

Row 14: (P2, k tbl) x 2, p2, k5, (p2, k tbl) x 2, p2.

Row 15: (K2, p tbl) x 2, k2, p5, (k2, p tbl) x 2, k2.

Row 16: (P2, k tbl) x 2, p2, dec 3, (p2, k tbl) x 2, p2.

Row 17: (K2, p tbl) x 2, k2, p3, (k2, p tbl) x 2, k2.

Row 18: (P2, k tbl) x 2, p2, sl1, k2tog, psso, (p2, k tbl) x 2, p2.

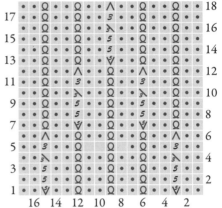

Bell and Rope

incto7 = p, k, p, k, p, k, p all into next stitch.

Row 1: P2, * k tbl, p2, yo, p2. Rep from *, k tbl, p2.

Row 2: K2, p tbl, * k2, incto7, k2, p tbl. Rep from *, k2.

Row 3: P2, * k tbl, p2, k5, k2tog, p2. Rep from *, k tbl, p2.

Row 4: K2, p tbl, * k2, p2tog, p4, k2, p tbl. Rep from *, k2.

Row 5: P2, * k tbl, p2, k3, k2tog, p2. Rep from *, k tbl, p2.

Row 6: K2, p tbl, * k2, p2tog, p2, k2, p tbl. Rep from *, k2.

Row 7: P2, * k tbl, p2, k1, k2tog, p2. Rep from *, k tbl, p2.

Row 8: K2, p tbl, * k2, p3 tog, k1, p tbl.

Rep from *, k2.

Row 9: P2, * k tbl, p4. Rep from *, k tbl, p2.

Row 10: K2, p tbl, * k4, p tbl. Rep from *, k2.

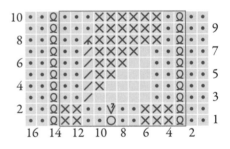

Nosegay

Multiple of 16.

Row 1 (WS): K7, p2, k7.

Row 2: P6, 1/1 RC, 1/1 LC, p6.

Row 3: K5, 1/1 LPC, p2, 1/1 RPC, k5.

Row 4: P4, 1/1 RPC, 1/1 RC, 1/1 LC, 1/1 LPC, p4.

Row 5: K3, 1/1 LPC, k1, p4, k1, 1/1 RPC, k3.

Row 6: P2, 1/1 RPC, p1, 1/1 RPC, k2, 1/1 LPC, p1, 1/1 LPC, p2.

Row 7: (K2, p1) x 2, k1, p2, k1, (p1, k2) x 2.

Row 8: P2, bobble, p1, 1/1 RPC, p1, k2, p1, 1/1 LPC, p1, bobble, p2.

Row 9: K4, p1, k2, p2, k2, p1, k4.

Row 10: P4, bobble, p2, k2, p2, bobble, p4.

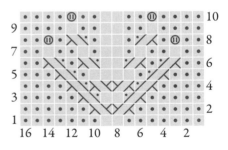

raised stitches

Lily of the Valley

Multiple of 27.

Bobble = k, p, k, p, k all into next stitch, pass 4th, 3rd, 2nd, 1st over last st.

Row 1 (WS): K2, p23, k2.

Row 2: P2, ssk, k6, (yo, k1) x 2, sl1, k2tog, psso, (k1, yo) x 2, k6, k2tog, p2.

Row 3: K2, p23, k2.

Row 4: P2, ssk, k5, yo, k1, yo, k2, sl1, k2tog, psso, k2, yo, k1, yo, k5, k2tog, p2.

Row 5: K2, p23, k2.

Row 6: P2, ssk, k4, yo, k1, yo, bobble, k2, sl1, k2tog, psso, k2, bobble, yo, k1, yo, k4, k2tog, p2.

Row 7: K2, p23, k2.

Row 8: P2, ssk, k3, yo, k1, yo, bobble, k3, sl1, k2tog, psso, k3, bobble, yo, k1, yo, k3, k2tog, p2.

Row 9: K2, p23, k2.

Row 10: P2, ssk, k2, yo, k1, yo, bobble, k4, sl1, k2tog, psso, k4, bobble, yo, k1, yo, k2, k2tog, p2.

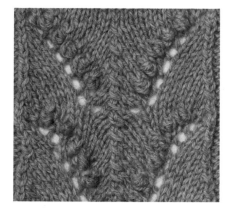

Row 11: K2, p23, k2.

Row 12: P2, ssk, (k1, yo) x 2, bobble, k5, sl1, k2tog, psso, k5, bobble, (yo, k1) x 2, k2tog, p2.

Row 13: K2, p23, k2.

Row 14: P2, ssk, yo, k1, yo, bobble, k6, sl1, k2tog, psso, k6, bobble, yo, k1, yo, k2tog, p2.

Loop Stitch

Elongated stitch = wrap yarn around needle as if to knit, then around middle finger of left hand two or three times, then back around needle and knit stitch. Replace stitch on left needle and knit again.

Row 1 (WS): K.

Row 2: P.

Row 3: (K1 elongated, k1) to end.

Row 4: P.

Row 5: (K1, k1 elongated) to end.

Row 6: P.

Row 7: (K1 elongated, k1) to end.

Row 8: K.

Row 9: P.

Row 10: K.

Repeat these 10 rows or Rows 1 to 8 for allover loops.

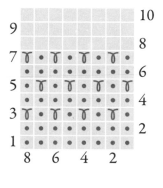

Indian Cross Stitch

Multiple of 8 plus 1.

Cross 8 = sl8 dropping extra loops; insert ln into first 4 sts and pass them over 2nd 4; return all sts to ln in that order and knit them one at a time.

Row 1: K.

Row 2: K.

Row 3: K.

Row 4: K.

Row 5: K1, (k1 elongated by wrapping yarn 4 times around needle) to end.

Row 6: Cross 8 to end, p1.

Row 7: K.

Row 8: K.

Row 9: K.

Row 10: K.

Row 11: K1, (k1 elongated) to end.

Row 12: Cross 4, (cross 8) to end, p1.

7

Raspberry Beret

I have used obvious bobbles for this beret, but wanted to avoid the finished piece looking like a Christmas Pudding! I did this by arranging the bobbles vertically. The purl and knit stitches in between the bobbles give the beret some stretch when worn. Bobbles, knots, tufts, and nupps are all different types of raised stitches and you could substitute any of them for the one I have used here.

Size
The beret is one size

Materials
2 x 1¾oz (50g) balls fuschia DK yarn
Size 3 (3.25mm) straight needles
Size 6 (4mm) straight needles

Gauge
22 sts and 28 rows – 4in (10cm) over st st

Bobble = MB: (k, p, k, p, k) all into next st. Turn, p5, turn, pass each st in turn over st nearest tip of needle.
Using smaller needles, cast on 121 sts and work 1½in (3cm) in k1, p1 rib, decreasing 1 st on last row (120 sts).
Change to larger needles.
Row 1: K2, * p3, MB, p3, K1. Rep from * ending p3, MB, k2.
Row 2: K2, * p5tog, k3, p1, k3. Rep from * ending p5tog, k3, k2.
Row 3: K2, * p3, k1. Rep from * ending k2.
Row 4: K2, * p1, k3. Rep from * ending k2 instead of k3.
Rep rows 1–4 twice more then rows 1–3 again.
Row 16: K twice in 1st stitch, k1 * p1, k1, k twice in next st, k1. Rep from *.
Row 17: K1, p2, * k1, p4, MB, p4. Rep from * ending k1, p4, MB, p2, k1.
Row 18: K3, p1, * k4, p1, k4. Rep from * ending k3.

Rows 19 & 20: Knit and purl as set.
Row 21 & 22: Rep Rows 17 & 18.
Row 23: K1, p2tog, * k1, p1, p2tog, p1, k1, p1, p2tog, p1. Rep from * ending p2tog, k1.
Row 24: Knit and purl as set.
Row 25: K1, p1, * p3tog, k1. Rep from * ending p1, k1.
Row 26: K2tog, * p1, k1. Rep from * ending k2tog.
Row 27: (P1, k1) to end, k1.
Row 28: (K1, p3tog) to end, k1.
Row 29: (P1, k1, p1, MB) to last 3, p1, k1, p1.
Row 30: (K1, p1, k1, p5tog) to last 3, k1, p1, k1.
Row 31: (P1, k1) to end, k1.
Row 32: (K1, p1) to end, k1.
Row 33: (P1, skpo) to end, p1, k2tog.
Thread yarn through remaining sts, draw up and fasten off leaving a long enough end to sew up back seam.

ALTERNATIVE STITCHES
You could substitute the bell and rope pattern on page 56 for the bobbles. It is a multiple of five and so would fit nicely into the same number of stitches. For a more allover textured effect, you could work the beret in the bud stitch on page 51.

LEFT: *The bobbles alternate with ribs that radiate out from the crown of the beret.*

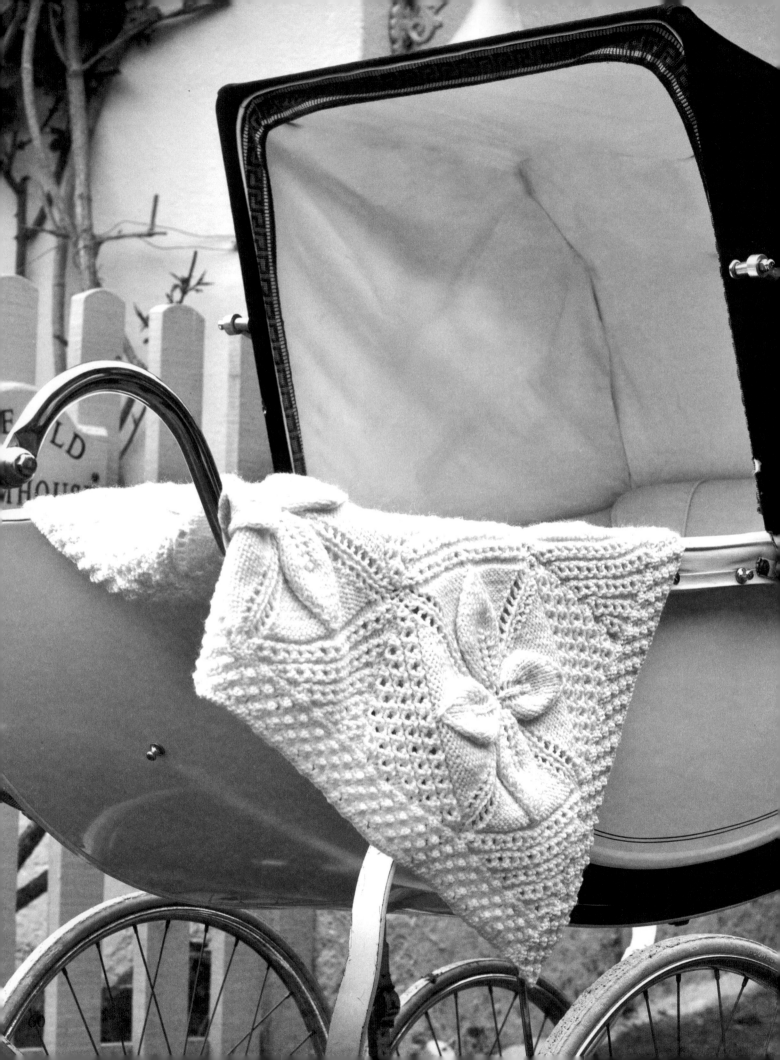

Heirloom Baby Blanket

The design for this pattern goes back as far as the 19th century and is often used to make up a blanket or counterpane. Essentially the blanket consists of a number of square blocks, where each is made up of four smaller squares. In this example, each of these four squares has a leaf in one corner which, when the larger blocks are assembled, meet at its center. The best way to join the squares is with mattress stitch, as it is easier to match the pattern when you have the right side facing you.

Size
The blanket measures approximately 24 x 34in (60 x 85cm)

Materials
7 x 1¾oz (50g) balls cream DK yarn
Size 7 (4.5mm) straight needles
Size 6 (4mm) straight needles
Tapestry needle

Gauge
Not important for this project

EACH SQUARE
Using larger needles, cast on 2sts.
Row 1: K1, yo, k1.
Row 2: P.
Row 3: (K1, yo) x 2, k1.
Row 4: P.
Row 5: (K1, yo) x 4, k1.
Row 6: P.
Row 7: K1, yo, p1, k2, yo, k1, yo, k2, p1, yo, k1.
Row 8: P2, k1, p7, k1, p2.
Row 9: K1, yo, p2, k3, yo, k1, yo, k3, p2, yo, k1.

Row 10: P2, k2, p9, k2, p2.
Row 11: K1, yo, p3, k4, yo, k1, yo, k4, p3, yo, k1.
Row 12: P2, k3, p11, k3, p2.
Row 13: K1, yo, p4, k5, yo, k1, yo, k5, p4, yo, k1.
Row 14: P2, k4, p13, k4, p2.
Row 15: K1, yo, p5, k6, yo, k1, yo, k6, p5, yo, k1.
Row 16: P2, k5, p15, k5, p2.
Row 17: K1, yo, p6, ssk, k11, k2tog, p6, yo, k1.
Row 18, P2, k6, p13, k6, p2.
Row 19: K1, yo, p7, ssk, p9, k2tog, p7, yo, k1.
Row 20: P2, k7, p11, k7, p2.
Cont as for last 2 rows, decreasing each side of leaf until there are 3 sts in leaf.
Row 29: K1, yo, p12, s1, k2tog, psso, p12, yo, k1.
Row 30: P.
Row 31: K1, yo, k to last st, yo, k1 (31sts).
Row 32: P.
Row 33: P.
Row 34: K2tog, * yo, k2tog. Rep from * ending yo, k3tog.
Row 35: P.
Row 36: P2tog, p to last 2sts, p2tog tbl.
Row 37: K.
Row 38: As for row 36.
Row 39: P.

Repeat rows 34 to 39 three more times, then rows 34 to 37 once.
P3tog.
Fasten off.
Make 24 squares and sew them together, to make six blocks of four with the leaves at center of each. Sew the blocks together to make a two-block by three-block panel.

THE BORDER
Using smaller needles, pick up and knit 112 sts along short edge of panel (28 sts per square) and knit 1 row.
Work 8 rows blackberry stitch.
Row 1: P.
Row 2: K1, * (k1, p1, k1) all into same stitch, p3tog. Rep from * ending k1.
Row 3: P.
Row 4: K1, * p3tog, (k1, p1, k1) all into same stitch. Rep from * ending k1.
Bind off p-wise.
Work opposite short edge to match.
Pick up and knit 190 sts along long edge of panel, 11 sts from each border and 28 sts from each square.
Knit 1 row then work as short edge.
Work opposite side to match.
Weave in all ends.

LEFT: *The photograph shows clearly how the four smaller squares join to make the larger one.*

Chapter Four
CABLE STITCHES

Relatively recent historically, the cable stitches of northern Europe go back some 200 years. Born of a necessity to protect against the elements in colder climates, these thick, chunky stitches were primarily used for making warm, dense, workwear fabrics. Many designs were inspired by ancient Celtic and Nordic art and are imbued with symbolism. Loved for their strong decorative impact and rich surface textures, the stitches have traveled far and wide and can now be found in a wide variety of knitting patterns.

Left Cross, Right Cross

Once the mainstay of the economy for a remote island people, cable knitting has become a global phenomenon. No longer reserved purely for robust workwear, these highly decorative stitches have found their way into many households in the forms of blankets, throws, and cushion covers.

Knitting cables involves crossing two or more stitches in order to produce a thicker, and therefore warmer, fabric. The origins of the technique can be seen in the twisted stitch knitting traditions of Bavaria in Germany, and those of the Tyrolean regions of northern Austria and Italy, where natural, cream-colored cable cardigans were decorated with colorful embroidery. Cable patterns then traveled to other temperate zones, where they were adopted and adapted among rural communities for producing thick, warm, workwear designed for protection against biting winds and cold weather.

The Aran Sweater

Among the best-known traditions of cable knitting, now practiced widely throughout the world is that of the Aran Islands off the west coast of Ireland, and which originally gained significance as a means of supporting local Irish people during the potato famine of the mid-19th century. Many families in Ireland lived on small crofts growing their own food, largely at subsistence level. Their main staple was the potato. When potato blight swept across the country between 1845 and 1851, it destroyed crops and many families struggled to survive. Women had always knitted stockings for themselves and their families and, as well as the typical blue gansey of the fishing communities (see page 13), a similar version in white, undyed wool for children to wear at their communion. Now the Irish government set up schools to teach people to knit more elaborate patterns into these sweaters, and to make them in adult sizes with a view to selling the garments to tourists.

The earliest pieces in Dublin's National Museum date from the 1930s. They were knitted in undyed, unwashed natural

wool, known locally as *bainin*, which best showed up the decorative cable patterns. The unwashed wool was spun by hand, a tradition that was maintained as recently as the 1970s among some Irish communities. Leaving the wool unwashed preserved the natural oils in it, so giving the knitted garments waterproof qualities.

As knitters became more skilled in their schooling, so the patterns became more complex. Some of the designs appear to be based on the intertwining motifs found in Celtic art; the lattice and cross stitch used in the Celtic Cardigan on pages 82–85 is one such motif.

ABOVE: *Taken in the mid-20th century, this photograph illustrates the humble home life of the inhabitants of the Aran Islands, who knitted elaborate pieces to sell to tourists.*
RIGHT: *Aran sweaters feature many permutations of different cables; in this example flying buttress, plait cables, and double ribbon stitch have been used in wide panels.*

While Aran sweaters are perhaps based on the T-shaped working garment of the fisherman, they are not traditionally knitted in the round, but worked in flat pieces. Sometimes the pattern on the back is different to that on the front, and the sleeves different again, although

RIGHT: *Knitting patterns appeared in publications as early as the mid-19th century, and yet cables did not feature on a wide scale until the mid-20th century.*

CROSS CABLE SWEATER

MATERIALS REQUIRED

8 ozs. of William Briggs' " Melody " 3-ply ; 2 buttons; one pair of No. 9 and one pair of No. 12 needles.

MEASUREMENTS

Length from shoulder to lower edge, 19½ ins. ; across under-arms (back and front), 17 ins. ; sleeve length from shoulder to lower edge, 24 ins.

TENSION (after Pressing)

15 st. to 2 ins.

BACK

** With No. 13 needles cast on 120 st. Rib 2½ ins., k. 1, p. 1, inc. 1 st. in every 12th st. of the last row only (120 st.). Change to No. 9 needles and the following pattern :—
1st row.—* P. 4, k. 6, repeat from * to end.
2nd row.—* P. 6, k. 4, repeat from * to end.
Repeat rows 1 and 2 twice more.
7th row.—* P. 4, slip next 3 st. on to spare needle and place in front of work. Knit next 3 st., knit the 3 st. from spare needle (this forms cable). Repeat from * to end.
8th row.—As 2nd row. Repeat rows 1 and 2 twice more.
13th row.—K. 5, * p. 4, k. 6, repeat from * ending p. 5.
14th row.—K. 5, * p. 6, k. 4, repeat from * ending p. 5.
Repeat rows 13 and 14 twice more.
19th row.—K. 5, * p. 4. Work cable, repeat (Continued on page 54)

BED JACKET

MATERIALS REQUIRED

6 ozs. of " Sirdar " 2-ply Super Shetland wool ; one pair of No. 8 and one pair of No. 12 needles ; 2 yards of ribbon.

MEASUREMENTS

Length from shoulder to lower edge, 20 ins.; across the back under-arms, 19 ins. ; across each front under-arm, 10 ins. ; sleeve length from shoulder to lower edge, 23½ ins.

TENSION

13 st. to 2 ins.

BACK

With No. 8 needles cast on 123 st.
1st row.—Knit 2, * m. 1, k. 3, sl. 1, k. 2 tog. p.s.s.o., k. 3, m. 1, k. 1, repeat from * ending p. 2.
2nd, 4th and 6th rows.—Purl.
3rd row.—K. 3, * m. 1, k. 2, sl. 1, k. 2 tog. p.s.s.o., k. 2, m. 1, k. 3, repeat from * to end.
5th row.—K. 1, k. 2 tog., * m. 1, k. 1, m. 1, k. 1, sl. 1, k. 2 tog. p.s.s.o., k. 1, m. 1, k. 1, m. 1, sl. 1, k. 2 tog. p.s.s.o., repeat from * ending m. 1, k. 2 tog., k. 1, instead of m. 1, sl. 1, k. 2 tog. p.s.s.o.
These 6 rows form pattern. Work until 11 ins. from the beg. of the cast-on edge.

SHAPE ARMHOLES

Cast off 10 st. at the beg. of the next 2 armhole end rows, then dec. 1 st. each end of every row until 73 st. remain. Work for 7 ins. on these 73 st.
(Continued on page 54)

36

ABBREVIATIONS

K. = knit ; p. = purl ; inc. = increase or increasing ; st. = stitch or stitches ; tog. = together ; beg. = beginning ; m. = make

---

retaining some of the motifs seen on the body. The central motif is usually the largest and is flanked by smaller cables, which can be followed either by another medium-sized cable, such as the lattice and cross stitch, or a wider panel of border stitches in honeycomb (see page 71) or a variety of moss stitch. A simple cable pattern is often used for the welt. Unlike the cables employed in fishermen's ganseys, which are typically four stitches wide and never more than six, these cables can cover panels several stitches wide, with the central one often measuring 5–6in (12–15cm).

Traditionally a working garment, the Aran sweater became a staple of the knitting tradition when American *Vogue* magazine published an article and a pattern for one in the 1950s, starting a trend that was copied in much of the Western world.

The Kilt Hose Tradition

Small cables, similar to those found in the Alpine regions, can be found on Scottish kilt hose, mainly around the top part of the stocking. By tradition, such stockings are turned over at the top, to conceal the garters that were used for holding them up in the days before elastic. The top part, or cuff, of the stocking was usually knitted first, in the round, with the right side facing the knitter. A deep panel of elastic rib would be knitted next, to assist the garter in keeping the stocking up once the top of the sock was folded over. With the rib section complete, this top section of the

stocking would be pushed down inside the needles and the rest of the work continued inside out. The leg section of the stocking might also feature a cable alternated with a wide rib.

While the early cables of the German "clock" sock tradition were typically two-stitch cables, those of the Scottish kilt hose tradition were more often of four- or six-stitch cables, used around the cuff and often on the leg too. The under and over Aran cable on page 68 or one of the versions of the claw pattern on page 72 are typical of the kinds of stitch use on the leg section, while the nautical cable stitch on page 76 or the basketweave cable on page 79 or would make interesting turnovers at the top.

Modern-day Cables

In recent times, the use of cables for decoration rather than warmth have gradually become more widespread. We have a tendency to look back to past traditions when looking for inspiration for designing clothing or textiles with which to fill our homes, and the cable patterns of the Aran tradition continue to find favor, albeit in modernized forms at times. Cables convey a comfortable, homely look and, today, it is not unusual to see cable patterns applied to many pieces designed for the home, such as the Cable Cushion Cover on pages 80–81, but also blankets, bedspreads, and throws of all sizes.

ABOVE: *What better use for cable stitches than making a fun tea cosy? A perfect means of keeping the pot warm.*
LEFT: *Kilts and knitted hose are a staple at the many highland games events that take place in Scotland throughout the year.*

Knitting Cables

The basic technique for knitting cables is to knit (or purl) more than one stitch in a different sequence to that on the left needle. In order to do this, a group of stitches is placed on a short, double-pointed needle, known as a cable needle and left behind or in front of the work, depending on the direction of the crossing —stitches left at the front of the work will slant to the left, stitches left at the back will slant to the right. The group of stitches on the knitting needle is worked first, followed by the stitches from the cable needle, which are then worked in the order given in the pattern instructions. This can include some purl stitches, which might entail the use of a second cable needle.

All cable patterns have a tendency to pull in widthwise, and although they can be any width—as can be seen from the Cable Cushion Cover—the wider they are, the more they will pull in. If you are working cables after a section of rib or stockinette stitch, therefore, you will need to increase one stitch for every four stitches in a cable to maintain the same width. When it comes to the end of the piece, you then decrease again by the same number before binding off.

STITCH VARIETIES

There is said to be a great deal of symbolism in cable stitches, many of which originated in poor, rural communities. The honeycomb represents hard work, for example, as in the honeybee; the tree of life is a good omen for a long life; the diamond mesh represents a fishing net and cables represent the ropes on the boats.

Many of these are represented in the rich collection of stitches that follows in the next few pages. As well as the most familiar cable designs, I have selected a few that were once fairly common among Aran knitters but appear to have fallen out of favor, and which I think are attractive enough to be restored. The interlocking twist on page 78 and the lattice and cross, both of which feature in the pattern for the Celtic Cardigan, are two of the more unusual examples.

Cable Stitches

Many cable stitches look complicated to work, but they are all achieved using the same basic technique: you simply knit (or purl) more than one stitch in a different order to that on the left needle. This results in a crossing of stitches, and it is this that forms the pattern. Some cables resemble braids or trelliswork, while others have similar motifs to those of textured stitches (see pages 14–23), for example, the honeycomb (pages 71 and 73) and diamond (page 76). Instructions for working cables can be found on page 142).

Chain Cable

Row 1: P3, 2/1/2 RC, p3.
Row 2: K3, p2, k1, p2, k3.
Row 3: P2, 2/1 RPC, k1, 2/1 LPC, p2.
Row 4: K2, p2, k3, p2, k2.
Row 5: P1, 2/1 RPC, p3, 2/1 LPC, p1.
Row 6: K1, p2, k5, p2, k1.
Row 7: P1, k2, p5, k2, p1.
Row 8: K1, p2, k5, p2, k1.
Row 9: P1, 2/1 LPC, p3, 2/1 RPC, p1.
Row 10: K2, p2, k3, p2, k2.
Row 11: P2, 2/1 LPC, p1, 2/1 RPC, p2.
Row 12: K3, p2, k1, p2, k3.

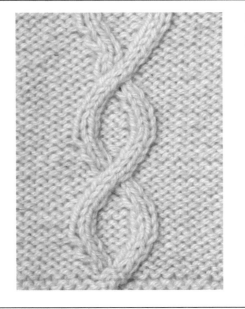

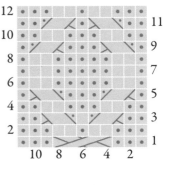

Under and Over Aran

Row 1: (P2, k2) x 3, p2.
Row 2: (K2, p2) x 3, k2.
Row 3: P2, 2/2/2 RPC, p2, k2, p2.
Row 4: (K2, p2) x 3, k2.
Row 5: (P2, k2) x 3, p2.
Row 6: (K2, p2) x 3, k2.
Row 7: (P2, k2) x 3, p2.
Row 8: (K2, p2) x 3, k2.
Row 9: P2, k2, p2, 2/2/2 LPC, p2.
Row 10: (K2, p2) x 3, k2.
Row 11: (P2, k2) x 3, p2.
Row 12: (K2, p2) x 3, k2.

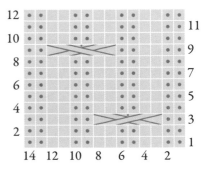

OXO

Row 1: P2, 2/2 LC, 2/2 RC, p2.
Row 2: K12.
Row 3: P2, k8, p2.
Row 4: K12.
Row 5: P2, k8, p2.
Row 6: K12.
Row 7: P2, 2/2 RC, 2/2 LC, p2.
Row 8: K12.
Row 9: P2, k8, p2.
Row 10: K12.
Row 11: P2, 2/2 RC, 2/2 LC, p2.
Row 12: K12.
Row 13: P2, k8, p2.
Row 14: K12.
Row 15: P2, 2/2 LC, 2/2 RC, p2.
Row 16: K12.

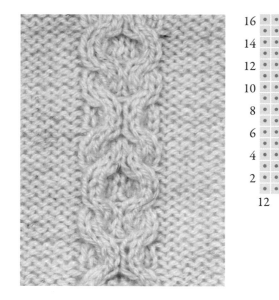

Alternate Cable

Row 1 (WS): (K2, p2)x 4, k2.
Row 2: (P2, k2) x 4, p2.
Row 3: (K2, p2) x 4, k2.
Row 4: (P2, k2) x 4, p2.
Row 5: (K2, p2) x 4, k2.
Row 6: (P2, k2) x 4, p2.
Row 7: (K2, p2) x 4, k2.
Row 8: (P2, k2) x 4, p2.
Row 9: [K2, p2) x 4, k2.
Row 10: P2, 2/2/2RC, (p2, k2) x 2, p2.
Row 11: (K2, p2) x 4, k2.
Row 12: (P2, k2) x 4, p2.
Row 13: (K2, p2) x 4, k2.
Row 14: (P2, k2) x 4, p2.
Row 15: (K2, p2) x 4, k2.
Row 16: (P2, k2) x 4, p2.
Row 17: (K2, p2) x 4, k2.
Row 18: (P2, k2) x 4, p2.
Row 19: (K2, p2) x 4, k2.
Row 20: (P2, k2) x 2, p2, 2/2/2LC, p2.

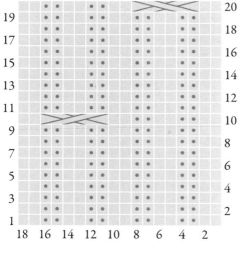

Nine-stitch Cable

Nine-stitch cable = sl3 to cn1 and hold at back, sl next 3 sts to cn2 and hold at front; k3, k3 from cn2, k3 from cn1.

Row 1: P2, k9, p2.
Row 2: K2, p9, k2.
Row 3: P2, k9, p2.
Row 4: K2, p9, k2.
Row 5: P2, nine-stitch cable, p2.
Row 6: K2, p9, k2.
Row 7: P2, k9, p2.
Row 8: K2, p9, k2.
Row 9: P2, k9, p2.
Row 10: K2, p9, k2.
Row 11: P2, k9, p2.
Row 12: K2, p9, k2.

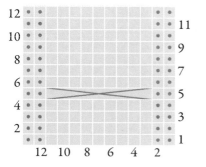

69

Ribbed Cable

12-stitch cable = sl next 6 onto cn and hold at back, k1 (p1, k1) twice, then (p1, k1) three times from cn.

Row 1: P2, (k tbl, p1) x 5, k tbl, p2.
Row 2: K2, (k tbl, k1) x 5, k tbl, k2.
Row 3: P1, 12-stitch cable, p2.
Row 4: K2, (k tbl, k1) x 5, k tbl, k2.
Row 5: P2, (k tbl, p1) x 5, k tbl, p2.
Row 6: K2, (k tbl, k1) x 5, k tbl, k2.
Row 7: P2, (k tbl, p1) x 5, k tbl, p2.
Row 8: K2, (k tbl, k1) x 5, k tbl, k2.
Row 9: P2, (k tbl, p1) x 5, k tbl, p2.
Row 10: K2, (k tbl, k1) x 5, k tbl, k2.
Row 11: P2, (k tbl, p1) x 5, k tbl, p2.
Row 12: K2, (k tbl, k1) x 5, k tbl, k2.
Row 13: P2, (k tbl, p1) x 5, k tbl, p2.
Row 14: K2, (k tbl, k1) x 5, k tbl, k2.

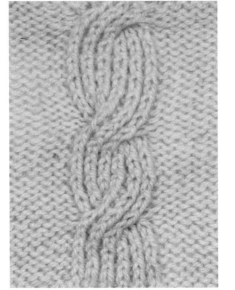

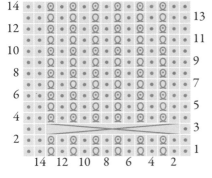

Wishbone and Seed

Row 1: P2, 1/3 RPC, 1/3 LPC, p2.
Row 2: K2, (p1, k1) x 3, p2, k2.
Row 3: P2, (k1, p1) x 3, k2, p2.
Row 4: K2, (p1, k1) x 3, p2, k2.
Row 5: P2, (k1, p1) x 3, k2, p2.
Row 6: K2, (p1, k1) x 3, p2, k2.
Row 7: P2, (k1, p1) x 3, k2, p2.
Row 8: K2, p1, k1, p3, k1, p2, k2.

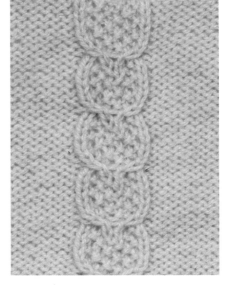

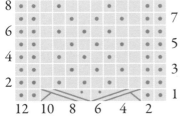

Medallion

Row 1: P2, k16, p2.
Row 2: K2, p16, k2.
Row 3: P2, 4/4RC, 4/4LC, p2.
Row 4: K2, p16, k2.
Row 5: P2, k16, p2.
Row 6: K2, p16, k2.
Row 7: P2, k16, p2.
Row 8: K2, p16, k2.
Row 9: P2, k16, p2.
Row 10: K2, p16, k2.
Row 11: P2, 4/4LC, 4/4RC, p2.
Row 12: K2, p16, k2.
Row 13: P2, k16, p2.
Row 14: K2, p16, k2.
Row 15: P2, k16, p2.
Row 16: K2, p16, k2.

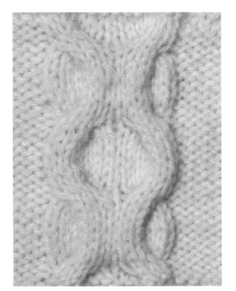

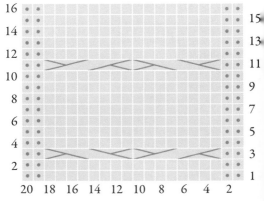

Medallion Moss

Row 1: K4, (p1, k1) x 2, p1, k4.
Row 2: P3, (k1, p1) x 2, k1, p5.
Row 3: K4, (p1, k1) x 2, p1, k4.
Row 4: P3, (k1, p1) x 2, k1, p5.
Row 5: 3/3 LC, k1, 3/3 RC.
Row 6: P13.
Row 7: K13.
Row 8: P13.
Row 9: K13.
Row 10: P13.
Row 11: K13.
Row 12: P13.
Row 13: 3/3 RC, k1, 3/3 LC.
Row 14: P3, (k1, p1) x 2, k1, p5.
Row 15: K4, (p1, k1) x 2, p1, k4.
Row 16: P3, (k1, p1) x 2, k1, p5.

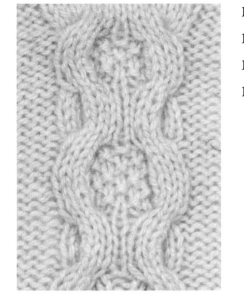

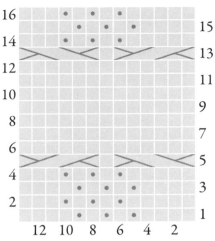

Hoof Prints

Multiple of 10.
Row 1: * P2, k2, p4, k2. Rep from *, p2, k2, p4, k2, p2.
Row 2: K2, p2, k4, p2, k2, * p2, k4, p2, k2. Rep from *.
Row 3: * P2, k2, p4, k2. Rep from *, p2, k2, p4, k2, p2.
Row 4: K2, p2, k4, p2, k2, * p2, k4, p2, k2. Rep from *.
Row 5: * P2, k2, p4, k2. Rep from *, p2, k2, p4, k2, p2.
Row 6: K2, p2, k4, p2, k2, * p2, k4, p2, k2. Rep from *.
Row 7: * P2, k2, p4, k2. Rep from *, p2, k2, p4, k2, p2.
Row 8: K2, p2, k4, p2, k2, * p2, k4, p2, k2. Rep from *.

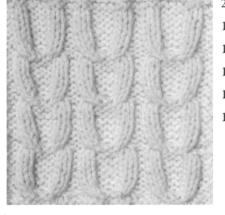

Row 9: * P2, 2/2 LC, 2/2 RC. Rep from *, p2, 2/2 LC, 2/2 RC, p2.
Row 10: K2, p2, k4, p2, k2, * p2, k4, p2, k2. Rep from *.

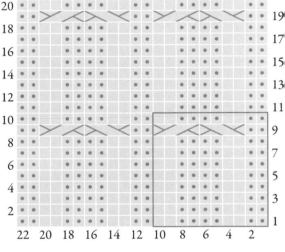

Honeycomb Cable

Row 1: K4, 1/1 RC, 1/1 LC, k4.
Row 2: K12.
Row 3: K2, (1/1 RC, 1/1 LC) x 2, k2.
Row 4: K12.
Row 5: (1/1 RC, 1/1 LC) x 3.
Row 6: K12.
Row 7: (1/1 LC, 1/1 RC) x 3.
Row 8: K12.
Row 9: K2, (1/1 LC, 1/1 RC) x 2, k2.
Row 10: K12.
Row 11: K4, 1/1 LC, 1/1 RC, k4.
Row 12: K12.

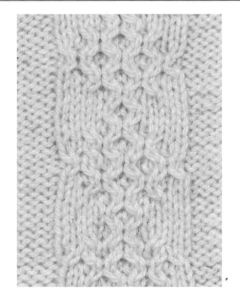

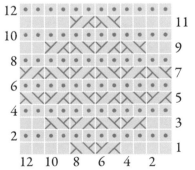

Trellis Cable

Row 1: P2, k2, p4, k2, p2.
Row 2: K2, p2, k4, p2, k2.
Row 3: P2, k2, p4, k2, p2.
Row 4: K2, p2, k4, p2, k2.
Row 5: (1/2 RPC, 1/2 LPC) x 2.
Row 6: P1, k4, p2, k4, p1.
Row 7: K1, p4, k2, p4, k1.
Row 8: P1, k4, p2, k4, p1.
Row 9: K1, p4, k2, p4, k1.
Row 10: P1, k4, p2, k4, p1.
Row 11: (1/2 LPC, 1/2 RPC) x 2.
Row 12: K2, p2, k4, p2, k2.
Row 13: P2, k2, p4, k2, p2.
Row 14: K2, p2, k4, p2, k2.

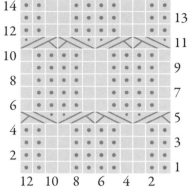

Diamond Panel

Row 1: P4, 1/1 RC, p4.
Row 2: K4, p2, k4.
Row 3: P3, 1/1 RPC, 1/1 LPC, p3.
Row 4: K3, p1, k2, p1, k3.
Row 5: P2, 1/1 RPC, p2, 1/1 LPC, p2.
Row 6: K2, p1, k4, p1, k2.
Row 7: P1, 1/1 RPC, p4, 1/1 LPC, p1.
Row 8: P2, k6, p1, k1.
Row 9: 1/1 RC, p6, 1/1 RC.
Row 10: K1, p1, k6, p1, k1.
Row 11: P1, 1/1 LPC, p4, 1/1 RPC, p1.
Row 12: K2, p1, k4, p1, k2.
Row 13: P2, 1/1 LPC, p2, 1/1 RPC, p2.
Row 14: K3, p1, k2, p1, k3.
Row 15: P3, 1/1 LPC, 1/1 RPC, p3.
Row 16: K4, p2, k4.

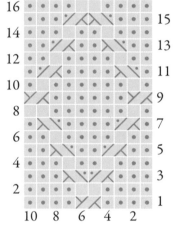

Claw Pattern

Up:
Row 1: K9.
Row 2: K9.
Row 3: 1/3 RC, k1, 1/3 LC.
Row 4: K9.

Down:
Row 1: K9.
Row 2: K9.
Row 3: 1/3 LC, k1, 1/3 RC.
Row 4: K9.

Small Honeycomb

Row 1: (2/2 RC, 2/2 LC) x 2.
Row 2: P16.
Row 3: K16.
Row 4: P16.
Row 5: (2/2 LC, 2/2 RC) x 2.
Row 6: P16.
Row 7: K16.
Row 8: P16.

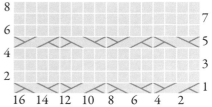

Slipped Chain

Row 1: P2, sl p-wise wyib, k5, sl p-wise wyib, p2.
Row 2: K2, sl p-wise wyif, p5, sl p-wise wyif, k2.
Row 3: P2, 1/2 LC, k1, 1/2 RC, p2.
Row 4: K2, p7, k2.
Row 5: P2, k2, sl p-wise wyib, k1, sl p-wise wyib, k2, p2.
Row 6: K2, p2, sl p-wise wyif, p1, sl p-wise wyif, p2, k2.
Row 7: P2, 1/2 RC, k1, 1/2 LC, p2.
Row 8: K2, p7, k2.

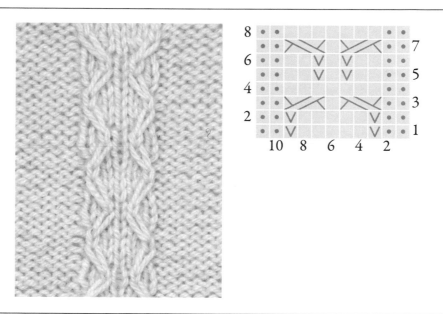

Garter Band

Row 1: P2, k2, p2, k4, p2, k2, p2.
Row 2: K2, p2, k2, p4, k2, p2, k2.
Row 3: P2, k2, p2, k4, p2, k2, p2.
Row 4: K2, p2, k2, p4, k2, p2, k2.
Row 5: P2, k2, p2, k4, p2, k2, p2.
Row 6: K2, p2, k2, p4, k2, p2, k2.
Row 7: P2, 4/2 RPC, 4/2 LPC, p2.
Row 8: K2, p2, k2, p4, k2, p2, k2.
Row 9: P2, k2, p2, k4, p2, k2, p2.
Row 10: K2, p2, k2, p4, k2, p2, k2.
Row 11: P2, k2, p2, k4, p2, k2, p2.
Row 12: K16.
Row 13: P2, k12, p2.
Row 14: K16.
Row 15: P2, k12, p2.
Row 16: K16.

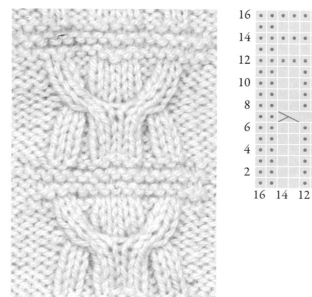

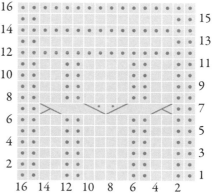

73

Hearts

incto7 = knit twice into horizontal strand before next stitch, (k1, p1, k1) all into next stitch, knit twice into following horizontal strand.

Row 1 (WS): P2, k7, p1, k7, p2.
Row 2: K2, p5, p2tog, incto7, p2tog, p5, k2.
Row 3: P2, k6, p3, k6, p2.
Row 4: 2/1 LPC, p3, p2tog, k1, incto7, k1, p2tog, p2, k1, 2/1 RPC.
Row 5: (K1, p2, k4, p2) x 2, k1.
Row 6: P1, 2/2 LPC, 2/2 RPC, k1, 2/2 LPC, 2/2 RPC, p1.
Row 7: K3, p4, k5, p4, k3.
Row 8: P3, 2/2 RPC, p5, 2/2 LPC, p3.
Row 9: K3, p2, k9, p2, k3.
Row 10: P1, 2/2 RPC, p9, 2/2 LPC, p1.
Row 11: K1, p2, k13, p2, k1.
Row 12: 2/1 RPC, p13, 2/1 LPC.

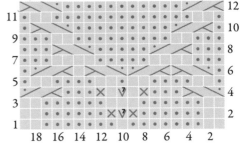

Wide Cable Panel

Row 1 (WS): P20.
Row 2: K6, 2/2 RC, 2/2 LC, k6.
Row 3: P20.
Row 4: K4, 2/2 RC, k4, 2/2 LC, k4.
Row 5: P20.
Row 6: K2, 2/2 RC, k8, 2/2 LC, k2.
Row 7: P20.
Row 8: 2/2 RC, k12, 2/2 LC.

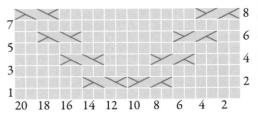

Staghorn Cable

Row 1: K4, 2/2 RC, 2/2 LC, k4.
Row 2: P16.
Row 3: K2, 2/2 RC, k4, 2/2 LC, k2.
Row 4: P16.
Row 5: 2/2 RC, k8, 2/2 LC.
Row 6: P16.

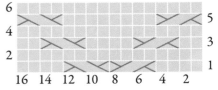

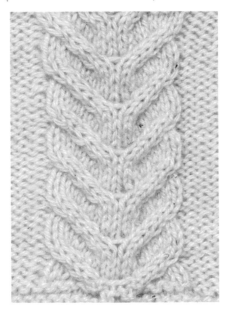

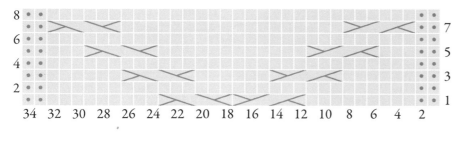

Wide Staghorn

Row 1: P2, k9, 3/3 RC, 3/3 LC, k9, p2.
Row 2: K2, p30, k2.
Row 3: P2, k6, 3/3 RC, k6, 3/3 LC, k6, p2.
Row 4: K2, p30, k2.
Row 5: P2, k3, 3/3 RC, k12, 3/3 LC, k3, p2.
Row 6: K2, p30, k2.
Row 7: P2, 3/3 RC, k18, 3/3 LC, p2.
Row 8: K2, p30, k2.

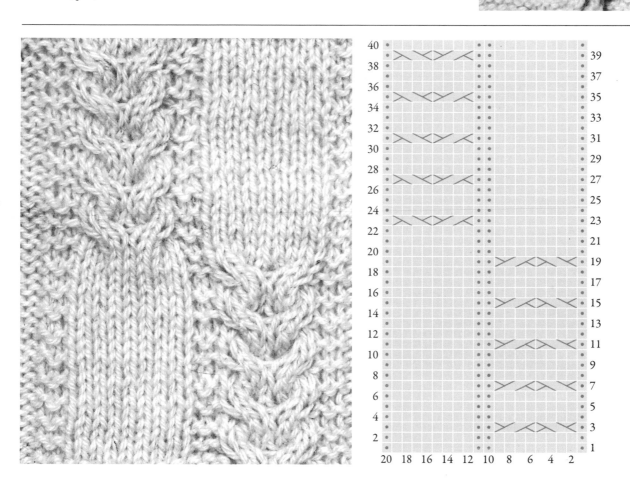

Staggered Horseshoe

Row 1: P1, k8, p2, k8, p1.
Row 2: K1, p8, k2, p8, k1.
Row 3: P1, 2/2 RC, 2/2 LC, p2, k8, p1.
Row 4: K1, p8, k2, p8, k1.
Row 5: P1, k8, p2, k8, p1.
Row 6: K1, p8, k2, p8, k1.
Row 7: P1, 2/2 RC, 2/2 LC, p2, k8, p1.
Row 8: K1, p8, k2, p8, k1.
Row 9: P1, k8, p2, k8, p1.
Row 10: K1, p8, k2, p8, k1.
Row 11: P1, 2/2 RC, 2/2 LC, p2, k8, p1.
Row 12: K1, p8, k2, p8, k1.
Row 13: P1, k8, p2, k8, p1.

Row 14: K1, p8, k2, p8, k1.
Row 15: P1, 2/2 RC, 2/2 LC, p2, k8, p1.
Row 16: K1, p8, k2, p8, k1.
Row 17: P1, k8, p2, k8, p1.
Row 18: K1, p8, k2, p8, k1.
Row 19: P1, 2/2 RC, 2/2 LC, p2, k8, p1.
Row 20: K1, p8, k2, p8, k1.
Row 21: P1, k8, p2, k8, p1.
Row 22: K1, p8, k2, p8, k1.
Row 23: P1, k8, p2, 2/2 RC, 2/2 LC, p1.
Row 24: K1, p8, k2, p8, k1.
Row 25: P1, k8, p2, k8, p1.
Row 26: K1, p8, k2, p8, k1.
Row 27: P1, k8, p2, 2/2 RC, 2/2 LC, p1.

Row 28: K1, p8, k2, p8, k1.
Row 29: P1, k8, p2, k8, p1.
Row 30: K1, p8, k2, p8, k1.
Row 31: P1, k8, p2, 2/2 RC, 2/2 LC, p1.
Row 32: K1, p8, k2, p8, k1.
Row 33: P1, k8, p2, k8, p1.
Row 34: K1, p8, k2, p8, k1.
Row 35: P1, k8, p2, 2/2 RC, 2/2 LC, p1.
Row 36: K1, p8, k2, p8, k1.
Row 37: P1, k8, p2, k8, p1.
Row 38: K1, p8, k2, p8, k1.
Row 39: P1, k8, p2, 2/2 RC, 2/2 LC, p1.
Row 40: K1, p8, k2, p8, k1.

Aran Diamond

Row 1: P3, 2/1 RC, p1, 2/1 LC, p3.
Row 2: K3, p3, k1, p3, k3.
Row 3: P2, 2/1 RC, p1, k1, p1, 2/1 LC, p2.
Row 4: K2, p3, k1, p1, k1, p3, k2.
Row 5: P1, 2/1 RC, (p1, k1) x 2, p1, 2/1 LC, p1.
Row 6: K1, p3, (k1, p1) x 2, k1, p3, k1.
Row 7: 2/1 RC, (p1, k1) x 3, p1, 2/1 LC.
Row 8: P3, (k1, p1) x 3, k1, p3.
Row 9: K2, (p1, k1) x 4, p1, k2.
Row 10: P2, (k1, p1) x 4, k1, p2.
Row 11: 1/2 LPC, (p1, k1) x 3, p1, 1/2 RPC.
Row 12: K1, p2, (k1, p1) x 3, k1, p2, k1.
Row 13: P1, 1/2 LPC, (p1, k1) x 2, p1, 1/2 RPC, p1.
Row 14: K2, p2, (k1, p1) x 2, k1, p2, k2.
Row 15: P2, 1/2 LPC, p1, k1, p1, 1/2 RPC, p2.
Row 16: K3, p2, k1, p1, k1, p2, k3.
Row 17: P3, 1/2 LPC, p1, 1/2 RPC, p3.
Row 18: K4, p2, k1, p2, k4.
Row 19: P4, 2/1/2 RPC, p4.
Row 20: K4, p5, k4.

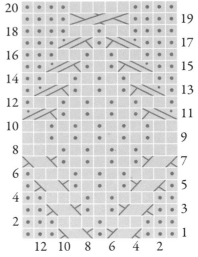

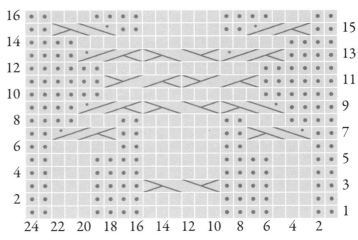

Nautical Cable

Row 1: P2, k3, p4, k6, p4, k3, p2.
Row 2: K2, p3, k4, p6, k4, p3, k2.
Row 3: P2, k3, p4, 3/3 LC, p4, k3, p2.
Row 4: K2, p3, k4, p6, k4, p3, k2.
Row 5: P2, k3, p4, k6, p4, k3, p2.
Row 6: K2, p5, k2, p6, k2, p5, k2.

Row 7: P2, 2/3 LPC, p2, k6, p2, 2/3 RPC, p2.
Row 8: K4, p3, k2, p6, k2, p3, k4.
Row 9: P4, 2/3 LPC, 3/3 LC, 2/3 RPC, p4.
Row 10: K6, p12, k6.
Row 11: P6, (3/3 RC) x 2, p6.
Row 12: K6, p12, k6.

Row 13: P4, 2/3 RPC, 3/3 LC, 2/3 RPC, p4.
Row 14: K4, p16, k4.
Row 15: K2, 2/3 RPC, p2, k6, p2, 2/3 LPC, p2.
Row 16: K2, p3, k4, p6, k4, p3, k2.

Half Diamond
Row 1: P2, k2, p4, k2, p1, k2, p4, k2, p2.
Row 2: K8, p2, k1, p2, k8.
Row 3: P8, 2/1/2 RPC, p8.
Row 4: K8, p2, k1, p2, k8.
Row 5: P7, 2/1 RPC, k1, 2/1 LPC, p7.
Row 6: K7, p2, k1, p1, k1, p2, k7.
Row 7: P6, 2/1 RPC, k1, p1, k1, 2/1 LPC, p6.
Row 8: K6, p2, (k1, p1) x 2, k1, p2, k6.
Row 9: P5, 2/1 RPC, (k1, p1) x 2, k1, 2/1 LPC, p5.
Row 10: K5, p2, (k1, p1) x 3, k1, p2, k5.
Row 11: P4, 2/1 RPC, (k1, p1) x 3, k1, 2/1 LPC, p4.
Row 12: K4, p2, (k1, p1) x 4, k1, p2, k4.
Row 13: P3, 2/1 RPC, (k1, p1) x 4, k1, 2/1 LPC, p3.
Row 14: K3, p2, (k1, p1) x 5, k1, p2, k3.

Row 15: P2, 2/1 RPC, (k1, p1) x 5, k1, 2/1 LPC, p2.
Row 16: K2, p2, (k1, p1) x 6, k1, p2, k2.

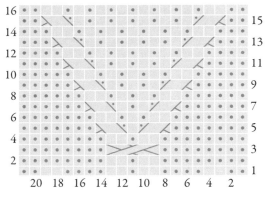

Nutcracker
Row 1 (WS): K6, p8, k6.
Row 2: P6, 2/2 RC, 2/2 LC, p6.
Row 3: K6, p8, k6.
Row 4: P4, 2/2 RPC, k4, 2/2 LPC, p4.
Row 5: K4, p2, k2, p4, k2, p2, k4.
Row 6: P2, (2/2 RPC) x 2, (2/2 LPC) x 2, p2.
Row 7: (K2, p2) x 2, k4, (p2, k2) x 2.
Row 8: (P2, k2) x 2, p4, (k2, p2) x 2.
Row 9: (K2, p2) x 2, k4, (p2, k2) x 2.
Row 10: P2, (2/2 LPC) x 2, (2/2 RPC) x 2, p2.
Row 11: K4, p2, k2, p4, k2, p2, k4.
Row 12: P4, 2/2 LPC, k4, 2/2 RPC, p4.

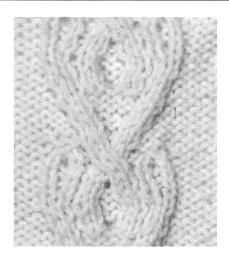

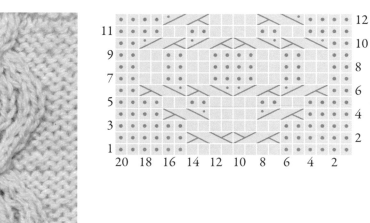

Valentine
Row 1: P5, 1/2 RPC, 1/2 LPC, p5.
Row 2: K5, p2, k2, p2, k5.
Row 3: P4, 1/2 RPC, p2, 1/2 LPC, p4.
Row 4: (K4, p2) x 2, k4.
Row 5: P3, 1/2 RPC, p4, 1/2 LPC, p3.
Row 6: K3, p2, k6, p2, k3.
Row 7: P2, (1/2 RPC) x 2, (1/2 LPC) x 2, p2.
Row 8: (K2, p2, k1, p2) x 2, k2.
Row 9: P1, (1/2 RPC) x 2, p2, (1/2 LPC) x 2, p1.
Row 10: (K1, p2) x 2, k4, (p2, k1) x 2.
Row 11: P1, k1, 1/1 LPC, 1/2 LPC, p2, 1/2 LPC, 1/1 RPC, k1, p1.
Row 12: (K1, p1) x 2, k1, p2, k2, p2, (k1, p1) x 2, k1.
Row 13: P1, k1, p1, 1/1 LPC, 1/2 LPC, 1/2 RPC, 1/1 RPC, p1, k1, p1.
Row 14: K1, p1, k2, p1, k1, p4, k1, p1, k2, p1, k1.

Row 15: P1, 1/1 LPC, 1/1 RPC, p1, 2/2 LC, p1, 1/1 LPC, 1/1 RPC, p1.
Row 16: K2, 1/1 RC, k2, p4, k2, 1/1 LC, k2.

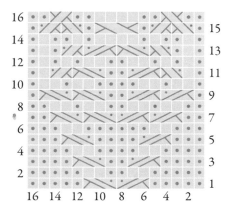

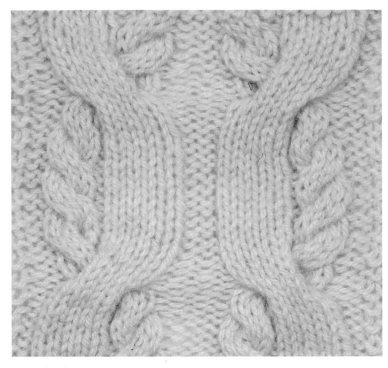

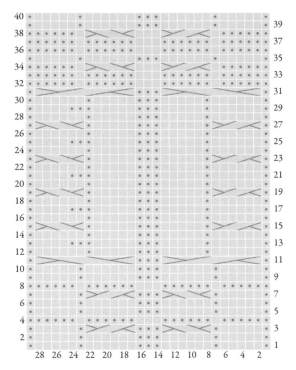

Interlocking Twist

Row 1: P1, k5, p1, k6, p3, k6, p1, k5, p1.
Row 2: K1, p5, k1, p6, k3, p6, k1, p5, k1.
Row 3: P1, k5, p1, 3/3LC, p3, 3/3RC, p1, k5, p1.
Row 4: K1, p5, k1, p6, k3, p6, k1, p5, k1.
Row 5: P1, k5, p1, k6, p3, k6, p1, k5, p1.
Row 6: K1, p5, k1, p6, k3, p6, k1, p5, k1.
Row 7: P1, k5, p1, 3/3LC, p3, 3/3RC, p1, k5, p1.
Row 8: K1, p5, k1, p6, k3, p6, k1, p5, k1.
Row 9: P1, k5, p1, k6, p3, k6, p1, k5, p1.
Row 10: K1, p5, k1, p6, k3, p6, k1, p5, k1.
Row 11: P1, 6/6RC, p3, 6/6LC, p1.
Row 12: K1, p6, k1, p5, k3, p5, k1, p6, k1.
Row 13: P1, k6, p1, k5, p3, k5, p3, k6, p1.
Row 14: K1, p6, k1, p5, k3, p5, k1, p6, k1.

Row 15: P1, 3/3RC, p1, k5, p3, k5, p1, 3/3LC, p1.
Row 16: K1, p6, k1, p5, k3, p5, k1, p6, k1.
Row 17: P1, k6, p1, k5, p3, k5, p3, k6, p1.
Row 18: K1, p6, k1, p5, k3, p5, k1, p6, k1.
Row 19: P1, 3/3RC, p1, k5, p3, k5, p1, 3/3LC, p1.
Row 20: K1, p6, k1, p5, k3, p5, k1, p6, k1.
Row 21: P1, k6, p1, k5, p3, k5, p3, k6, p1.
Row 22: K1, p6, k1, p5, k3, p5, k1, p6, k1.
Row 23: P1, 3/3RC, p1, k5, p3, k5, p1, 3/3LC, k1.
Row 24: K1 , p6, k1, p5, k3, p5, k1, p6, k1.
Row 25: P1, k6, p1, k5, p3, k5, p3, k6, p1.
Row 26: K1, p6, k1, p5, k3, p5, k1, p6, k1.
Row 27: P1, 3/3RC, p1, k5, p3, k5, p1, 3/3LC, p1.

Row 28: K1, p6, k1, p5, k3, p5, k1, p6, k1.
Row 29: P1, k6, p1, k5, p3, k5, p3, k6, p1.
Row 30: K1, p6, k1, p5, k3, p5, k1, p6, k1.
Row 31: P1, 6/6LC, p3, 6/6RC, p1.
Row 32: K1, p5, k1, p6, k3, p6, k1, p5, k1.
Row 33: P1, k5, p1, k6, p3, k6, p1, k5, p1.
Row 34: K1, p5, k1, p6, k3, p6, k1, p5, k1.
Row 35: P1, k5, p1, 3/3LC, p3, 3/3RC, p1, k5, p1.
Row 36: K1, p5, k1, p6, k3, p6, k1, p5, k1.
Row 37: P1, k5, p1, k6, p3, k6, p1, k5, p1.
Row 38: K1, p5, k1, p6, k3, p6, k1, p5, k1.
Row 39: P1, k5, p1, 3/3LC, p3, 3/3RC, p1, k5, p1.
Row 40: K1, p5, K1, P6, K3, P6, K1, P5, k1.

Celtic Cable

Row 1: P2, (M1 left leaning, M1 right leaning, p4) x 2, M1 left leaning, M1 right leaning, p2.
Row 2: K2, (p4, k4) x 2, p4, k2.
Row 3: P2, (k1, M1 left leaning, M1 right leaning, k1, p4) x 2, k1, M1 left leaning, M1 right leaning, k1, p2.
Row 4: K2, (p4, k4) x 2, p4, k2.
Row 5: (2/2 RPC, 2/2 LPC) x 3.
Row 6: P2, (k4, p4) x 2, k4, p2.
Row 7: K2, (p4, 2/2 LC) x 2, p4, k2.
Row 8: P2, (k4, p4) x 2, k4, p2.
Row 9: (2/2 LPC, 2/2 RPC) x 3.
Row 10: K2, (p4, k4) x 2, p4, k2.
Row 11: P2, (2/2 RC, p4) x 2, 2/2 RC, p2.
Row 12: K2, (p4, k4) x 2, p4, k2.
Row 13: (2/2 RPC, 2/2 LPC) x 3.
Row 14: P2, (k4, p4) x 2, k4, p2.

Row 15: K2, (p4, 2/2 LC) x 2, p4, k2.
Row 16: P2, (k4, p4) x 2, k4, p2.
Row 17: (2/2 LPC, 2/2 RPC) x 3.
Row 18: K2, (p4, k4) x 2, p4, k2.

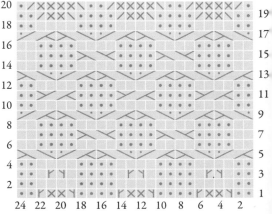

Row 19: P2, (ssk, k2tog, p4) x 2, ssk, k2tog, p2.
Row 20: K1, (k2tog, ssk, k2) x 2, k2tog, ssk, k1.

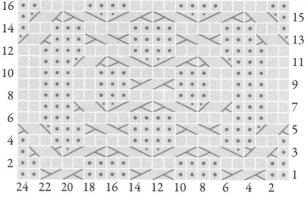

Danish Cable

Row 1: P2, (2/2 RC, p4) x 2, 2/2 RC, p2.
Row 2: K2, (p4, k4) x 2, p4, k2.
Row 3: P1, 2/1 RC, (2/2 LPC, 2/2 RPC) x 2, 2/1 LC, p1.
Row 4: K1, p2, k3, p4, k4, p4, k3, p2, k1.
Row 5: 2/1 RPC, p3, 2/2 LC, p4, 2/2 LC, p3, 2/1 LPC.

Row 6: P2, k3, p5, k4, p5, k3, p2.
Row 7: K2, p3, 2/1 RPC, 2/2 LPC, 2/2 RPC, 2/1 LPC, p3, k2.
Row 8: (P2, k3) x 2, p4, (k3, p2) x 2.
Row 9: (K2, p3) x 2, 2/2 RC, (p3, k2) x 2.
Row 10: (P2, k3) x 2, p4, (k3, p2) x 2.
Row 11: K2, p3, 2/1 LPC, 2/2 RPC, 2/2 LPC, 2/1 RPC, p3, k2.

Row 12: P2, (k4, p4) x 2, k4, p2.
Row 13: 2/1 LPC, p3, 2/2 LC, p4, 2/2 LC, p3, 2/1 RPC.
Row 14: K1, p2, k3, p4, k4, p4, k3, p2, k1.
Row 15: P1, 2/1 LPC, (2/2 RPC, 2/2 LPC) x 2, 2/1 RPC, p1.
Row 16: K2, (p4, k4) x 2, p4, k2.

Celtic Plait

Row 1: K3, (p4, k6) x 2, p2.
Row 2: K2, (p6, k4) x 2, p3.
Row 3: K3, (p4, 3/3 LC) x 2, p2.
Row 4: K2, (p6, k4) x 2, p3.
Row 5: (2/3 LPC, 2/3 RPC) x 2, 2/3 LPC.
Row 6: P3, (k4, p6) x 2, k2.
Row 7: P2, (3/3 RPC, p4) x 2, k3.
Row 8: K2, (p6, k4) x 2, p3.
Row 9: (2/3 RPC, 2/3 LPC) x 2, 2/3 RPC.
Row 10: K2, (p6, k4) x 2, p3.

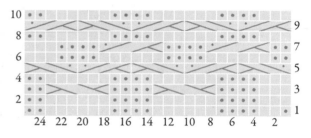

Basketweave

Round 1: K12.
Round 2: K12.
Round 3: K12.
Round 4: K12.
Round 5: K12.
Round 6: (3/3 RC) x 2.
Round 7: K12.
Round 8: K12.
Round 9: K12.
Round 10: K12.
Round 11: K12.
Round 12: K3, * 3/3 LC, k3. Rep from *.

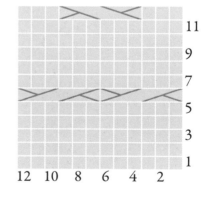

Cable Cushion Cover

Many designs that employ cables, use more than one type in combination, as is the case with the motifs I have chosen for this cushion. The wide cable at the center of the red panel is simply a large version of a rope cable, separated by two purl stitches. The cables either side of it are staghorn cables (see page 74). The white section of the cushion is made from a textured fabric, which complements the knitting.

Size
The cushion measures 16 x 16in (40 x 40cm)

Materials
39in (1m) fabric
1 x 15in (38cm) zipper
1 x 1¾oz (50g) ball red aran yarn
Size 7 (4.5mm) straight needles
Stuffing or cushion pad for 16 x 16in
(40 x 40cm) cushion

Gauge
18 sts and 26 rows – 4in (10cm)
on size 7 (4.5mm) needles over st st

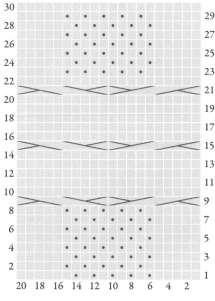

Cable Pattern 2

CABLE PATTERN 1
(Right and left cables)
Row 1: K6, p1, k6.
Row 2: P6, k1, p6.
Row 3: K6, p1, k6.
Row 4: P6, k1, p6.
Row 5: 3/3 RC, p1, 3/3 LC.
Row 6: P6, k1, p6.
Row 7: K6, p1, k6.
Row 8: P6, k1, p6.

CABLE PATTERN 2
(Center cable)
Row 1: K5, (p1, k1) x 4, p1, k6.
Row 2: P5, (k1, p1) x 4, k1, p6.
Row 3: K5, (p1, k1) x 4, p1, k6.
Row 4: P5, (k1, p1) x 4, k1, p6.
Row 5: K5, (p1, k1) x 4, p1, k6.
Row 6: P5, (k1, p1) x 4, k1, p6.
Row 7: K5, (p1, k1) x 4, p1, k6.
Row 8: P5, (k1, p1) x 4, k1, p6.
Row 9: 5/5 RC, 5/5 LC.
Row 10: P20.
Row 11: K20.
Row 12: P20.
Row 13: K20.
Row 14: P20.
Row 15: 5/5 RC, 5/5 LC.
Row 16: P20.
Row 17: K20.
Row 18: P20.
Row 19: K20.
Row 20: P20.
Row 21: 5/5 RC, 5/5 LC.
Row 22: P20.
Row 23: K6, (p1, k1) x 4, p1, k5.
Row 24: P6, (k1, p1) x 4, k1, p5.
Row 25: K6, (p1, k1) x 4, p1, k5.
Row 26: P6, (k1, p1) x 4, k1, p5.
Row 27: K6, (p1, k1) x 4, p1, k5.
Row 28: P6, (k1, p1) x 4, k1, p5.
Row 29: K6, (p1, k1) x 4, p1, k5.
Row 30: P20.

Using red yarn, cast on 86 sts.
Knit 1 row, purl 1 row.
Next row: P12, Cable Pattern 1, p8, Cable
Pattern 2, p8, cable pattern 1, p12.
Continue for 30 rows.
Work 1 row knit.
Bind off.

FRONT COVER
Measure your piece of knitting. Cut two
pieces of fabric to the same width and to
equal 17½in (44cm) in length when all three
pieces are assembled as in the photograph.
With right sides facing and taking ½in (1cm)
seams, stitch the three pieces together.

FINISHING
For the back cover, cut a piece of fabric 16½in
(42cm) long and 2½in (5cm) wider than the
front cover. With right sides facing, center the
front cover on the back cover, squaring it so
that the back cover folds round to the front
slightly (see photograph). Taking ½in (1cm)
seams, sew side seams followed by bottom
seam. Turn cover right sides out and insert
cushion pad. Turn in ½in (1cm) seams at the
top and sew or insert a zipper.

ALTERNATIVE STITCHES
*The large, central cable in this pattern could
be replaced with a single column of the
nutcracker on page 77, while medallion moss
on page 71 and Aran diamond on page 76
would make equally lovely side cables.*

Celtic Cardigan

Any combination of twists and cables will make a beautiful piece of knitting, which is why Aran knits have a timeless beauty, just as fashionable today as they were more than 200 years ago. I have chosen to use some familiar and some less well known cables in this project. The interlocking twist (see page 78) is a repetitive design that is not difficult to follow, while the lattice and cross, though more complex, is easily achieved by the competent knitter.

Size

The cardigan is ladies' bust sizes:
28–30 (32–34, 36–38, 40–42) in/
71–76 (81–86, 91.5–96.5, 101.5–106.5) cm

Materials

9 (10, 12, 14) x 1¾oz (50g) balls
turquoise DK yarn
Size 6 (4mm) straight needles
Size 3 (3.25mm) straight needles
7 buttons

Gauge

28 sts = 4in (10cm) on size 6 (4mm)
needles over st st

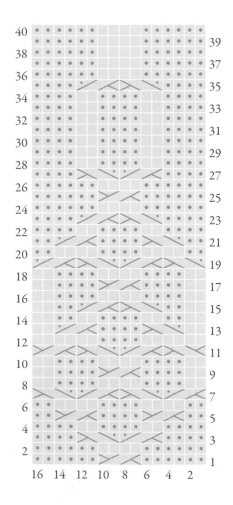

LATTICE AND CROSS PATTERN
Row 1: P6, 2/2LC, p6.
Row 2: K6, p4, k6.
Row 3: P4, 2/2RC, 2/2LC, p4.
Row 4: K4, p2, k4, p2, k4.
Row 5: P2, 2/2RC, p4, 2/2LC, p2.
Row 6: K2, p4, k4, p4, k2.
Row 7: 2/2RC, 2/2LC, 2/2RC, 2/2LC.
Row 8: P2, k4, p4, k4, p2.
Row 9: K2, p4, 2/2RC, p4, k2.
Row 10: P2, k4, p4, k4, p2.
Row 11: 2/2LC, 2/2RC, 2/2LC, 2/2RC.
Row 12: P6, k4, p6.
Row 13: K2, 2/2LC, p4, 2/2RC, k2.
Row 14: P2, k2, p2, k4, p2, k2, p2.
Row 15: K2, p2, 2/2LC, 2/2RC, p2, k2.
Row 16: P2, k4, p4, k4, p2.
Row 17: K2, p4, 2/2RC, p4, k2.
Row 18: P2, k4, p4, k4, p2.
Row 19: 2/2RC, 2/2LC, 2/2RC, 2/2LC.
Row 20: K2, p4, k4, p4, k2.

Row 21: P2, 2/2RC, p4, 2/2LC, p2.
Row 22: K4, p2, k4, p2, k4.
Row 23: P4, 2/2RC, 2/2LC, p4.
Row 24: K6, p4, k6.
Row 25: P6, 2/2LC, p6.
Row 26: K6, p4, k6.
Row 27: P4, 2/2RC, 2/2LC, p4.
Row 28: K4, p2, k4, p2, k4.
Row 29: P4, k2, p4, k2, p4.
Row 30: K4, p2, k4, p2, k4.
Row 31: P4, k2, p4, k2, p4.
Row 32: K4, p2, k4, p2, k4.
Row 33: P4, k2, p4, k2, p4.
Row 34: K4, p2, k4, p2, k4.
Row 35: P4, k2, p4, k2, p4.
Row 36: K4, p2, k4, p2, k4.
Row 37: P4, k2, p4, k2, p4.
Row 38: K4, p2, k4, p2, k4.
Row 39: P4, 2/2RC, 2/2LC, p4.
Row 40: K6, p4, k6.

GULLWING PATTERN
Row 1: K2, s2, k2.
Row 2: P2, s2, p2.
Row 3: Lift 3rd st and knit it, work 4th st at front on cn, k next 2 sts, then k st from front.
Row 4: P6.

ABOVE: *The interlocking twist cables frame the buttons when the cardigan is fastened.*

INTERLOCKING TWIST PATTERN

Row 1: K5, p1, k6, p3, k6, p1, k5.
Row 2: P5, k1, p6, k3, p6, k1, p5.
Row 3: K5, p1, 3/3LC, p3, 3/3RC, p1, k5.
Row 4: P5, k1, k6, k3, p6, k1, p5.
Row 5: K5, p1, k6, p3, k6, p1, k5.
Row 6: P5, k1, p6, k3, p6, k1, p5.
Row 7: K5, p1, 3/3LC, p3, 3/3RC, p1, k5.
Row 8: P5, k1, p6, k3, p6, k1, p5.
Row 9: K5, p1, k6, p3, k6, p1, k5.
Row 10: P5, k1, p6, k3, p6, k1, p5.
Row 11: 6/6RC, p3, 6/6LC.
Row 12: P6, k1, p5, k3, p5, k1, p6.
Row 13: K6, p1, k5, p3, k5, p3, k6.
Row 14: P6, k1, p5, k3, p5, k1, p6.
Row 15: 3/3RC, p1, k5, p3, k5, p1, 3/3LC.
Row 16: P6, k1, p5, k3, p5, k1, p6.
Row 17: K6, p1, k5, p3, k5, p3, k6.
Row 18: P6, k1, p5, k3, p5, k1, p6.
Row 19: 3/3RC, p1, k5, p3, k5, p1, 3/3LC.
Row 20: P6, k1, p5, k3, p5, k1, p6.
Row 21: K6, p1, k5, p3, k5, p3, k6.
Row 22: P6, k1, p5, k3, p5, k1, p6.
Row 23: 3/3RC, p1, k5, p3, k5, p1, 3/3LC.
Row 24: P6, k1, p5, k3, p5, k1, p6.
Row 25: K6, p1, k5, p3, k5, p3, k6.
Row 26: P6, k1, p5, k3, p5, k1, p6.
Row 27: 3/3RC, p1, k5, p3, k5, p1, 3/3LC.
Row 28: P6, k1, p5, k3, p5, k1, p6.
Row 29: K6, p1, k5, p3, k5, p3, k6.
Row 30: P6, k1, p5, k3, p5, k1, p6.
Row 31: 6/6LC, p3, 6/6RC.
Row 32: P5, k1, p6, k3, p6, k1, p5.
Row 33: K5, p1, k6, p3, k6, p1, k5.
Row 34: P5, k1, p6, k3, p6, k1, p5.
Row 35: K5, p1, 3/3LC, p3, 3/3RC, p1, k5.
Row 36: P5, k1, p6, k3, p6, k1, p5.
Row 37: K5, p1, k6, p3, k6, p1, k5.
Row 38: P5, k1, p6, k3, p6, k1, p5.
Row 39: K5, p1, 3/3LC, p3, 3/3RC, p1, k5.
Row 40: P5, k1, p6, k3, p6, k1, p5.

CABLE PATTERN FOR LEFT FRONT

Moss 3 (5, 9, 5) (k1, p1, k1 on RS), p1
(2, 1, 3), Gullwing 6, p1 (2, 3, 3), 3/3RC
every 6th row, p1 (2, 3, 3), Lattice and Cross
16, p1 (2, 3, 3), 3/3LC every 6th row, p1
(2, 3, 3), Interlocking Twist 14, p2. (58 (65,
72, 79) sts). Reverse for right front.

CABLE PATTERN FOR BACK

Work as for left and right front, using
only 1 purl stitch to separate the two
interlocking cables, so:
Moss 3 (5, 9, 5), p1 (2, 1, 3), Gullwing, p1
(2, 3, 3), 3/3RC, p1 (2, 3, 3), Lattice and
Cross, p1 (2, 3, 3), 3/3LC, p1 (2, 3, 3),
Interlocking Twist, p1, Interlocking Twist,
p1(2, 3, 3), 3/3RC, p1 (2, 3, 3), Lattice
and Cross, p1(2, 3, 3), 3/3LC, p1(2, 3, 3),
gullwing, p1(2, 1, 3), moss 3 (5, 9, 5). (113
(127, 141, 155) sts).

CABLE PATTERN FOR SLEEVES

Moss 3 (7, 9, 5), p1, Gullwing 6, p1 (1, 2, 2),
* 3/3RC, p1 (1, 2, 2), repeat from * 0 (0, 0, 1)
more times, Lattice and Cross 16, p1 (1, 2, 2),
* 3/3LC, p1(1, 2, 2), repeat from * 0 (0, 0, 1)
more times, gull wing 6, p1, moss 3 (7, 9, 5)
(52 (60, 68, 76) sts).

BACK

Cast on 113 (127, 141, 155) sts on larger
needles and work foundation row of
cable pattern. Continue following charts/
instructions until piece measures 12 (12½, 13,
14) in/30.5 (31.75, 33, 35.5) cm.
Armhole shaping: Cast off 5 (6, 8, 8) sts at
beginning of next 2 rows. Dec 1 st at each end
of every alternate row until 93 (99, 105, 115)
sts remaining.
Work straight until armhole measures 7½
(8¼, 8¾, 9¼) in/19 (21, 22, 23.5) cm.

Shoulder shaping: Cast off 13 (14, 15, 17) sts
at beginning of next 4 rows. 41 (43, 45, 47)
sts remaining for back of neck. Place sts on
holder.

RIGHT FRONT

Cast on 58 (65, 72, 79) sts on larger
needles and work foundation row of the
cable pattern.
Continue following charts/instructions until
work measures same as back to armholes.
Armhole: Dec for armhole at right end, as
for back. Continue until armhole measures
5 (5½, 6, 6) in/12.75 (14, 15.25, 15.25) cm
with 48 (51, 54, 59) sts remaining, ending
with a right side row.
Shape neck: Wrong side of work facing.
Work 40 (43, 45, 50) sts. Slip last 8 (8, 9, 9)
sts to holder.
Next row: Dec 1 st at neck edge (left end)
every row 14 (15, 15, 16) times, until 26 (28,
30, 34) sts remain.
Work evenly until armhole measures same as
back to shoulder, ending with a wrong side row.
Bind off 13 (14, 15, 17) sts at beg next and
foll alt row.
Left cardigan front: Work as for right side,
reversing shapings.

SLEEVES

Cast on 49 (53, 57, 61) sts on smaller
needles. Work in k1, p1 ribbing for
2in (5cm).
Inc 3 sts evenly across the row to 52
(56, 60, 64) sts total.
Change to larger needles and work the
cable pattern.
Inc 1 st at each end of every 5th row once,
then every 6th row 15 (17, 19, 21) times to
84 (92, 100, 108) sts bringing extra sts into
moss stitch.

ALTERNATIVE STITCHES

*If you want to substitute any of the cables
used here you will probably have to adjust
the number of stitches. For example, if using
a cable with 14 stitches in each panel—for
example, the under and over Aran cable
on page 68—you would need to work an
extra purl stitch at each side of one of the
other cables in the pattern.*

Continue until sleeve measures 17 (17¾, 18¼, 18¾) in/43 (45, 46.5, 47.5) cm.
Shape cap: Bind off 6 (6, 6, 8) sts at beg of next two rows (72 (80, 88, 92) sts rem).
Dec 1 st at each end of every row 6 (7, 6, 8) times, then dec 1 st at each end of every 2nd row 11 (13, 19, 17) times, then dec 1 st at each end of every row 6 (7, 6, 8) times.
Bind off remaining 26 sts loosely.

SHOULDER SEAMS
Sew fronts to back along shoulder seams.

NECKBAND
With right side of work facing, slip 8 (8, 9, 9) sts from right front neck holder onto smaller needle, pick up and knit 21 (26, 29, 32) sts from right front neck edge, 41 (43, 45, 47) sts from back neck holder, 21 (26, 29, 32) sts from left front neck edge and 8 (8, 9, 9) sts from left front neck holder. Total 99 (111, 121, 129) sts.
Work 6 rows in k1, p1 ribbing.
Bind off loosely.

FRONT BANDS
Using smaller needles, pick up and knit 101 (105, 109, 115) sts along right front edge.
Work 3 rows k1, p1 rib.
Buttonhole row: Rib 4 (6, 4, 4), (bind off 3, rib 10 (10, 11, 12)) seven times, bind off 3, rib to end.
Work 4 more rows rib, casting on 3 sts over those bound off.
Bind off.
Work left front band to match, omitting the buttonholes.

FINISHING
Set in sleeves.
Join side and sleeve seams.
Sew on buttons.

Chapter Five
LACE STITCHES

Fine lace knitting has a history that goes back several centuries, to the households of European royalty and nobility. Today, heirloom pieces can be found in the knitting traditions of countries across the globe, where the finest homespun yarns were used to make delicate, intricately patterned stockings and shawls. In stark contrast to the heavily textured workwear often made within the same communities, such pieces were designed for special occasions, such as christenings, weddings, and other times of great celebration.

Yarn Over

Lace knitting was once the preserve of only the very wealthy, with trends in Europe set by late-16th-century royalty. Over the years, the tradition has filtered through generations of rural communities, producing garments that have come to define regional costume throughout Europe.

It is thought that lace-knitting traditions began in Spain, in an attempt to copy the fine thread laces made mainly in the convents of Europe during the 16th and 17th centuries. Although the earliest mention of lace knitting is around 1840, owing to the intricacy of the work, it is very likely that knitters were using the technique long before this.

Lace-knitting Methods

The technique involves knitting a sequence of holes and decreases, which are balanced throughout the piece so that the pattern begins and ends with the same number of stitches. The frequency of the holes, made by taking the yarn over or around the needle before forming the next stitch, determines how open the final piece is. Sometimes the holes are made on just a few rows, giving the impression of little flowers, diamonds, or Vs dotted over the work. They can also be made on every row, which produces an extremely fine and delicate fabric referred to by some as knitted lace, rather than lace knitting.

From Regal to Rural

Traditional lace knitting is most often associated with the intricate knitted stockings that originated in France towards the end of the 16th century. Henri II wore a pair of hand-knitted silk stockings for his wedding in 1559, and Queen Elizabeth I was presented with a

ABOVE: *Wool, silk, and cotton were almost always spun by hand, by women and children. In many rural communities, spinning by hand continued long after mechanization.*

pair of diamond patterned stockings by Mrs Montague, her silk mistress, several years later.

As the technique spread, it became a popular craft in many other countries, particularly those in which a fine enough fiber could be spun—for example, among the people of the Portuguese islands of the Azores, where lace shawls and stockings were made from the fine-spun fiber of the aloe plant. The patterns from many of these articles were later copied by knitters in Berlin and Vienna

to produce delicate, round, lace-knitted doilies and table mats.

Passing from one generation to the next, lace-knitting techniques were later used among many folk communities to produce traditional garments, such as lacy patterned white stockings and delicate knitted shawls. Examples of such pieces are common to many regions, most notably the Shetland Isles to the northeast of Scotland, the Danish Faroe Isles, Estonia in the Baltic region of Europe, and Orenburg in Russia.

The Shetland Islands
In the Shetland Islands lace knitting started in the 1840s, when steamer services between the islands and the mainland began. The service attracted visitors from all parts of the world and many of the islanders discovered that their knitting was popular with the tourists. Unst, the most northerly island, produced a very finely spun yarn ideally suited to knitting lace. It was plucked by hand from the neck of the sheep, after which it was spun by an expert spinner. The knitted shawls made from this wool were especially highly prized. Some were so fine that even a 50in (125cm) square could be drawn through a wedding ring.

Such shawls had no visible cast-on and bind-off edges, adding to the soft texture for which they were renowned.

The Shetland shawl tradition continues largely unchanged today. Each is made in one piece on several double-pointed needles, or a long circular needle. Some are knitted from the center outwards, with stitches picked up for an inner border and then an outer border knitted on afterwards. For others, the outer border is knitted first and then stitches are picked up from there and the shawl knitted in towards the center.

Of the stitches demonstrated in this book, snowflake lace, open diamonds, and Madeira lace on pages 95 and 98 are ideal for a square-knitted center, with fountain lace, fern lace, or one of the horseshoe laces on pages 101 and 103 making good choices for wide borders. Thicker wool, often handspun using a drop spindle, were used for making the everyday shawls that the women of Shetland wore. The Hap Shawl on pages 106–109 is inspired by such pieces.

Each knitter had her own way of making a shawl, but almost all had a border of the old shale stitch on page 99. Some shawls were made all in one color, while others had bands of different

ABOVE: *Shetland shawls are handwashed and blocked before use, often using an age-old method of stretching a shawl over a pegged frame and leaving it to dry naturally.*

natural shades introduced into the borders. I have chosen to use some dyed colors, but traditionally the wool would be varying shades of cream and brown. Incidentally, "hap" is an old Scots word meaning to cover or wrap up warmly.

Icelandic Shawls
There is a close similarity between Shetland hap shawls and the triangular shawls of Iceland. The Icelandic shawls were always made on a background of stockinette stitch and knitted either from three or four stitches at the top, which were increased at the center and each end, or worked from a lower border of old shale, horseshoe or similar pattern and then gradually decreased at the center and sides of the shawl to give a wide triangular shape.

The central portion of the triangle was worked in a simple allover pattern such as the open diamond lace or the spider stitch on page 97 and then a wide border of old shale, horseshoe, or similar pattern would be knitted in different

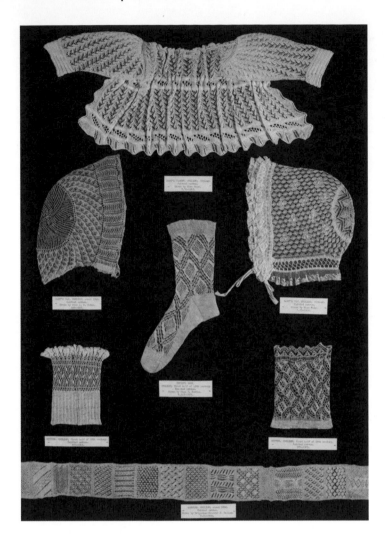

LEFT: *A collection of exquisite pieces made using lace knitting techniques and dating from around 1800. At the bottom of the selection, is a long sampler, where each newly discovered stitch has been added in turn.*
RIGHT: *A young bride from Orenburg, Russia, demonstrates the fine quality of her shawl by drawing it through her wedding ring.*

shades of the local wool. Finally the outer edges of the shawl would be finished off with crochet chain loops, or a further elaborate lacy border would be worked.

Similar Shawl Traditions

Shawls from other parts of the world were also made with wool fine enough to be drawn through a ring. The Russian Orenburg shawl is made from a mixture of silk and fine mohair. The shawls are square or rectangular, with geometric stitch patterns such as diamonds or V shapes. Like Shetland shawls, they have a central pattern with a wider border and a scalloped edging. The main difference is that Orenburg shawls are worked on a stockinette stitch background.

Elsewhere, Estonian and Faroese shawls use allover garter stitch, while Shetland shawls can be either, or a mixture of the two. Some of the stitch patterns are the same, for example, old shale, but this can look slightly different depending on the ground stitch. Those from Estonia are made using similar lace stitches but with the addition of nupps (small bobbles) in the fabric, similar to those found in the lily of the valley pattern on page 57. However, the traditional way of making them is not in one piece but as a long central portion, onto which separate edgings are sewn once the center is complete.

Samplers and Stitches

Printed patterns for lace stitches were not available to knitters in the way that they are now. Instead, knitters made samplers comprising stitches that had been handed down through the family, or that they had made up for themselves by studying an existing piece of lacework. These samplers were often made like a long scarf and were easily rolled up to be carried with the knitter wherever they went. Many women who emigrated to the American colonies would have taken their lace samplers with them and there are several on display in American museums.

A number of the stitches in the pages that follow would have been very familiar to those used by knitters of the 19th century, particularly the cat's face rib on page 92, spider stitch, the diamond leaf lace on page 94, fern lace, and the variations of the old shale pattern.

Many of the patterns that feature are fairly international, based as they are on obvious geometric progressions, but others, such as print o' the wave on page 100 and old shale are specific to Shetland. Many of the diamond patterns are variations on the patterns for French stockings, while those resembling leaves or other natural forms are Dutch.

The lace edging of the Lacy Socks on pages 104–105 is a horseshoe lace pattern. This is another pattern that has several variations, all of which would be simple to adapt as the natural progression of the stitches can easily be seen. It is one of the classic Shetland lace patterns and was often used as an alternative to old shale in the borders of a shawl.

Lace Stitches

Lace stitches are made by knitting a sequence of holes and decreases that are balanced throughout a piece so that the pattern begins and ends with the same number of stitches. The frequency of the holes, made by taking the yarn over or around the needle before forming the next stitch, determines how open the final piece is. Sometimes the holes are made on just a few rows, giving the impression of little flowers, diamonds, or V's dotted over the piece. Or they can be made on every row, which produces an extremely fine and delicate fabric.

Cat's Face Rib
Multiple of 9.
Row 1: K1, * p2, k1, k2tog, yo twice, ssk, k1, p1. Rep from *, p1, k1.
Row 2: K2, * k1, p3, ptbl, p2, k2. Rep from *, k1.
Row 3: K1, * p2, k2tog, yo, k2, yo, ssk, p1. Rep from *, p1, k1.
Row 4: K2, * k1, p6, k2. Rep from *, k1.
Row 5: K1, * p2, k6, p1.Rep from *, p1, k1.
Row 6: K2, * k1, p6, k2.Rep from *, k1.

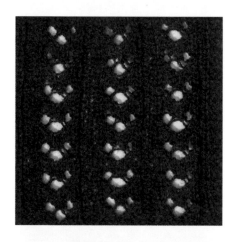

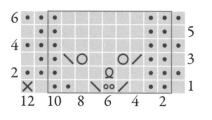

Ribbed Lace
Row 1: * P2, k2, yo, k1, ssk, Rep from *, p2.
Row 2: K2, * p5, k2. Rep from *.
Row 3: * P2, k2tog, k1, yo, k2. Rep from *, p2.
Row 4: K2, * p5, k2. Rep from *.

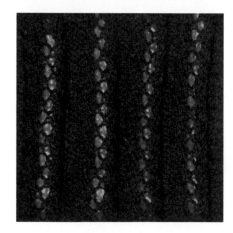

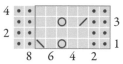

Ribbed Leaves

Row 1: P2, k4, k2tog, yo, p2.
Row 2: K2, p6, k2.
Row 3: P2, k3, k2tog, k1, yo, p2.
Row 4: K2, p6, k2.
Row 5: P2, yo, ssk, k4, p2.
Row 6: K2, p6, k2.
Row 7: P2, yo, k1, ssk, k3, p2.
Row 8: K2, p6, k2.

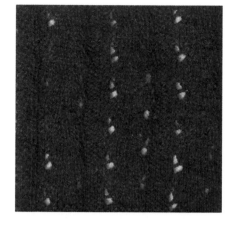

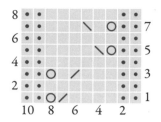

Tilting Block

Row 1: (Ssk, yo) x 4, k8.
Row 2: K9, p7.
Row 3: (Ssk, yo) x 4, k8.
Row 4: K9, p7.
Row 5: (Ssk, yo) x 4, k8.
Row 6: K9, p7.
Row 7: (Ssk, yo) x 4, k8.
Row 8: K9, p7.
Row 9: K8, (yo, k2tog) x 4.
Row 10: P7, k9.
Row 11: K8, (yo, k2tog) x 4.
Row 12: P7, k9.
Row 13: K8, (yo, k2tog) x 4.
Row 14: P7, k9.
Row 15: K8, (yo, k2tog) x 4.
Row 16: P7, k9.

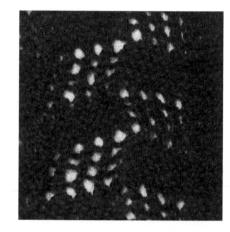

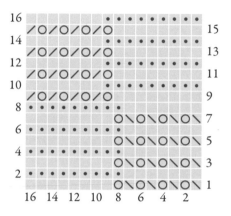

Crystal and Pearl

Row 1: P8.
Row 2: K8.
Row 3: P8.
Row 4: P1, (p2tog tbl, yo) x 3, p1.
Row 5: K8.
Row 6: P2, (p2tog tbl, yo) x 2, p2.
Row 7: K8.
Row 8: P3, p2tog tbl, yo, p3.
Row 9: K8.
Row 10: P2, (p2tog tbl, yo) x 2, p2.
Row 11: K8.
Row 12: P1, (p2tog tbl, yo) x 3, p1.

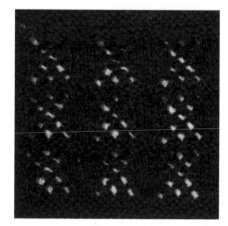

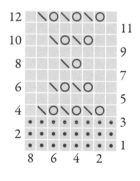

Arbor

Row 1: K1, yo, k2, ssk, p7, k2tog, k2, yo, k1.
Row 2: P5, k7, p5.
Row 3: K2, yo, k2, ssk, p5, k2tog, k2, yo, k2.
Row 4: P6, k5, p6.
Row 5: K2tog, yo, k1, yo, k2, ssk, p3, k2tog, k2, yo, k2tog, yo, k1.
Row 6: P7, k3, p7.
Row 7: K1, k2tog, yo, k1, yo, k2, ssk, p1, k2tog, k2, yo, k2tog, yo, k2.
Row 8: P8, k1, p8.
Row 9: P4, k2tog, k2, yo, k1, yo, k2, ssk, p4.
Row 10: K4, p9, k4.
Row 11: P3, k2tog, k2, yo, k2tog, yo, k1, yo, k2, ssk, p3.
Row 12: K3, p11, k3.
Row 13: P2, k2tog, k2, (yo, k2tog) x 2, yo, k1, yo, k2, ssk, p2.
Row 14: K2, p13, k2.

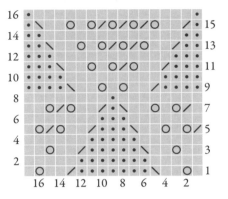

Row 15: P1, k2tog, k2, (yo, k2tog) x 3, yo, k1, yo, k2, ssk, p1.
Row 16: K1, p15, k1.

Coral Lace

Multiple of 10.
Row 1: (WS) P.
Row 2: K1, * k1, k2tog, (k1, yo) x 2, k1, ssk, k2. Rep from *.
Row 3: P.
Row 4: K1, * k2tog, k1, yo, k3, yo, k1, ssk, k1. Rep from *.
Row 5: P.
Row 6: K1, * k1, yo, k5, yo, k1, sl1, k2tog, psso. Rep from *.
Row 7: P.
Row 8: K1, * yo, k1, ssk, k3, k2tog, k1, yo, k1. Rep from *.
Row 9: P.
Row 10: K1, * k1, yo, k1, ssk, k1, k2tog, k1, yo, k2. Rep from *.
Row 11: P.

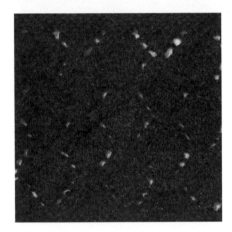

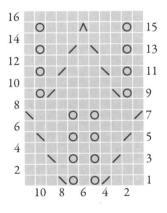

Row 12: K1, * k2, yo, k1, sl1, k2tog, psso, k1, yo, k3. Rep from *.

Diamond Leaf

Row 1: K3, k2tog, yo, k1, yo, ssk, k3.
Row 2: P11.
Row 3: K2, k2tog, (k1, yo) x 2, k1, ssk, k2.
Row 4: P11.
Row 5: K1, k2tog, k2, yo, k1, yo, k2, ssk, k1.
Row 6: P11.
Row 7: K2tog, k3, yo, k1, yo, k3, ssk.
Row 8: P11.
Row 9: K1, yo, ssk, k5, k2tog, yo, k1.
Row 10: P11.
Row 11: K1, yo, k1, ssk, k3, k2tog, k1, yo, k1.
Row 12: P11.
Row 13: K1, yo, k2, ssk, k1, k2tog, k2, yo, k1.
Row 14: P11.
Row 15: K1, yo, k3, sl1, k2tog, psso, k3, yo, k1.
Row 16: P11.

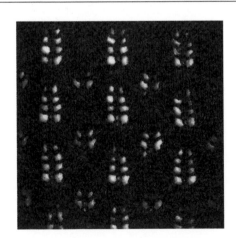

Snowflake

Row 1 (WS): P13.
Row 2: * K4, ssk, yo, k1, yo, k2tog.
Rep from *, k4.
Row 3: P13.
Row 4: * K5, yo, sl2, k1, p2sso, yo, k1.
Rep from *, k4.
Row 5: P13.
Row 6: * K4, ssk, yo, k1, yo, k2tog.
Rep from *, k4.
Row 7: P13.
Row 8: * Ssk, yo, k1, yo, k2tog, k3, ssk.
Rep from *, yo, k1, yo, k2tog.
Row 9: P13.
Row 10: * K1, yo, sl2, k1, p2sso, yo, k5.
Rep from *, yo, sl2, k1, p2sso, yo, k1.
Row 11: P13.

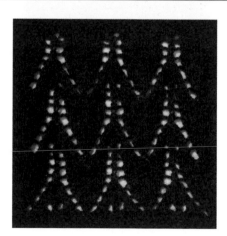

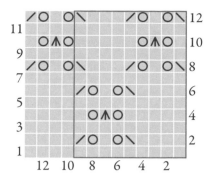

Row 12: * Ssk, yo, k1, yo, k2tog, k3, ssk.
Rep from *, yo, k1, yo, k2tog.

Open Diamonds

Row 1: K1, yo, ssk, k5, k2tog, yo, k1.
Row 2: P2, yo, p2tog, k3, p2tog tbl, yo, p2.
Row 3: K3, yo, ssk, k1, k2tog, yo, k3.
Row 4: K3, p1, yo, p3 tog, yo, p1, k3.
Row 5: K3, k2tog, yo, k1, yo, ssk, k3.
Row 6: K2, p2tog tbl, yo, p3, yo, p2tog, p1, k1.
Row 7: K1, k2tog, yo, k5, yo, ssk, k1.
Row 8: P2tog tbl, yo, p1, k5, p1, yo, p2tog.

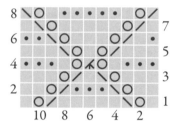

Pointed Chevron

Row 1 (WS): P11.
Row 2: (K1, yo, ssk, k2tog, yo) x 2, k1.
Row 3: P11.
Row 4: K2, yo, ssk, k3, k2tog, yo, k2.
Row 5: P11.
Row 6: K3, yo, ssk, k1, k2tog, yo, k3.
Row 7: P11.
Row 8: K4, yo, sl1, k2tog, psso, yo, k4.
Row 9: P11.
Row 10: K1, ssk, k2, yo, k1, yo, k2, k2tog, k1.
Row 11: P11.
Row 12: K1, ssk, k2, yo, k1, yo, k2, k2tog, k1.
Row 13: P11.
Row 14: K1, ssk, k2, yo, k1, yo, k2, k2tog, k1.

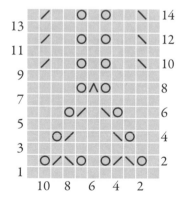

Strawberry

Row 1: Ssk, k4, yo, k1, yo, k4, ssk.
Row 2: P2tog, (p3, yo) x 2, p3, p2tog.
Row 3: Ssk, k2, yo, k5, yo, k2, ssk.
Row 4: P2tog, p1, yo, p7, yo, p1, p2tog.
Row 5: Ssk, yo, k9, yo, ssk.
Row 6: P1, yo, p4, p3 tog, p4, yo, p1.
Row 7: K2, yo, k3, sl1, k2tog, psso, k3, yo, k2.
Row 8: P3, yo, p2, p3 tog, p2, yo, p3.
Row 9: K4, yo, k1, sl1, k2tog, psso, k1, yo, k4.
Row 10: P5, yo, p3 tog, yo, p5.

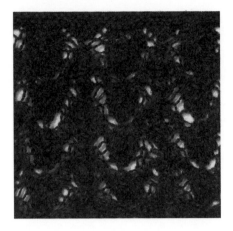

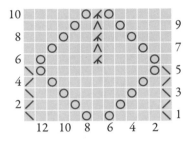

Small Arrow

Row 1 (WS): P7.
Row 2: K3, yo, ssk, k2.
Row 3: P7.
Row 4: K1, k2tog, yo, k1, yo, ssk, k1.
Row 5: P7.
Row 6: K2tog, yo, k3, yo, ssk.
Row 7: P7.
Row 8: K1, yo, ssk, k1, k2tog, yo, k1.
Row 9: P7.
Row 10: K1, yo, ssk, k1, k2tog, yo, k1.

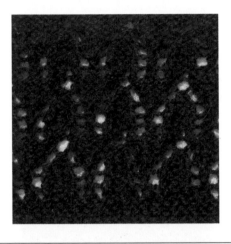

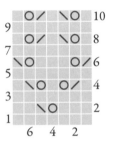

Falling Leaves

Row 1: K1, * yo, k3, k3tog, k3, yo, k1. Rep from *, k1. Rep from *, k3, k2tog.
Row 2: P.
Row 3: K1, * k1, yo, k2, k3tog, k2, yo, k2. Rep from *, yo. Rep from *, k3, k2tog.
Row 4: P.
Row 5: K1, * k2, yo, k1, k3tog, k1, yo, k3. Rep from *, k1. Rep from *, k1, yo, k1, k2tog.
Row 6: P.
Row 7: K1, * k3, yo, k3tog, yo, k4. Rep from *, k1. Rep from *, k2, yo, k2tog.
Row 8: P.
Row 9: Ssk, * k3, yo, k1, yo, k3, k3tog. Rep from *, k1. Rep from *, k2, yo, k1.
Row 10: P.
Row 11: Ssk, * k2, yo, k3, yo, k2, k3tog. Rep from *, k1. Rep from *, k1, yo, k2.
Row 12: P.
Row 13: Ssk, * k1, yo, k5, yo, k1, k3tog. Rep from *, yo. Rep from *, k4.
Row 14: P.

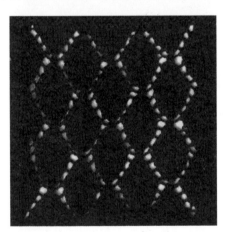

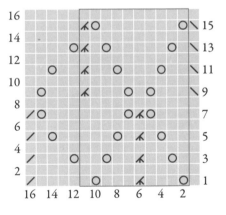

Row 15: Ssk,* yo, k7, yo, k3tog. Rep from *, k1. Rep from *, k4.
Row 16: P.

Spider Stitch

Row 1 (WS): P7.
Row 2: K1, yo, ssk, k1, k2tog, yo, k1.
Row 3: P7.
Row 4: K1, yo, ssk, k1, k2tog, yo, k1.
Row 5: P7.
Row 6: K1, yo, ssk, k1, k2tog, yo, k1.
Row 7: P7.
Row 8: K2, yo, sl1, k2tog, psso, yo, k2.
Row 9: P7.
Row 10: K1, k2tog, yo, k1, yo, ssk, k1.
Row 11: P7.
Row 12: K2tog, yo, k3, yo, ssk.

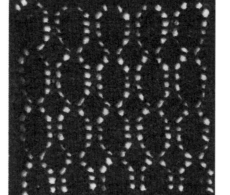

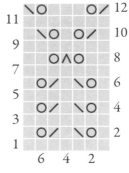

English Lace

Multiple of 9.
Row 1 (WS): P9.
Row 2: K1, * k2, yo, sl1, k2tog, psso, yo, k3.
Rep from *.
Row 3: * P2, yo, p2tog, p1, p2tog tbl, yo, p1.
Rep from *, p1.
Row 4: K1, * yo, ssk, yo, sl1, k2tog, psso, yo,
k2tog, yo, k1. Rep from *.
Row 5: * P2, yo, p2tog, p1, p2tog tbl, yo, p1.
Rep from *, p1.
Row 6: K1, * k2, yo, sl1, k2tog, psso, yo, k3.
Rep from *.
Row 7: P9.
Row 8: K2tog, * yo, k5, yo, sl1, k2tog, psso.
Rep from *.
Row 9: * P1, p2tog tbl, yo, p3, yo, p2tog. Rep
from *, p1.
Row 10: K2tog, * yo, k2tog, yo, k1, yo, ssk, yo,
sl1, k2tog, psso ; repeat from *.

Row 11: * P1, p2tog tbl, yo, p3, yo, p2tog. Rep
from *, p1.
Row 12: K2tog, * yo, k5, yo, sl1, k2tog, psso.
Rep from *.

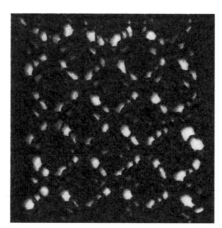

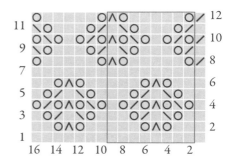

Alternating Leaf

Multiple of 9.
Row 1: K15.
Row 2: P15.
Row 3: * K6, k2tog, k1, yo. Rep from *, k6.
Row 4: P6, * p1, yo, p1, p2tog, p5. Rep from *.
Row 5: * K4, k2tog, k1, yo, k2. Rep from *, k6.
Row 6: P6, * p3, yo, p1, p2tog, p3. Rep from *.
Row 7: K15.
Row 8: P15.
Row 9: * Yo, k1, ssk, k6. Rep from *, yo, k1,
ssk, k3.
Row 10: P2, p2tog tbl, p1, yo, p1, * p5, p2tog
tbl, p1, yo, p1. Rep from *.
Row 11: * K2, yo, k1, ssk, k4. Rep from *, k2,
yo, k1, ssk, k1.
Row 12: P2tog tbl, p1, yo, p3, * p3, p2tog tbl,
p1, yo, p3. Rep from *.

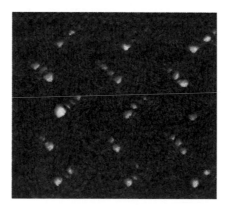

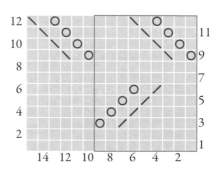

Slanting Leaves

Row 1: P1, k11, p1.
Row 2: P13.
Row 3: P1, k11, p1.
Row 4: P13.
Row 5: P1, (k1, yo) x 2, k2tog, k1, ssk, k4, p1.
Row 6: P13.
Row 7: P1, k2, yo, k1, yo, k2tog, k1, ssk, k3, p1.
Row 8: P13.
Row 9: P1, k3, yo, k1, yo, k2tog, k1, ssk, k2, p1.
Row 10: P13.
Row 11: P1, k4, yo, k1, yo, k2tog, k1, ssk, k1, p1.
Row 12: P13.

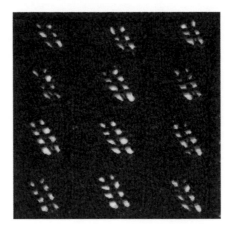

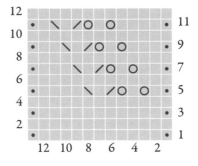

Madeira

Row 1: K3, yo, ssk, k5.
Row 2: P10.
Row 3: K2, yo, sl1, k2tog, psso, yo, k5.
Row 4: P10.
Row 5: K1, yo, ssk, k1, k2tog, yo, k4.
Row 6: P10.
Row 7: K2, yo, sl1, k2tog, psso, yo, k5.
Row 8: P10.
Row 9: Yo, ssk, k3, k2tog, yo, k3.
Row 10: P10.
Row 11: K1, yo, ssk, k1, k2tog, yo, k4.
Row 12: P10.
Row 13: K2, yo, sl1, k2tog, psso, yo, k5.
Row 14: P10.
Row 15: K8, yo, ssk.
Row 16: P10.
Row 17: K7, yo, sl1, k2tog, psso, yo.
Row 18: P10.
Row 19: Yo, k5, yo, ssk, k1, k2tog.
Row 20: P10.
Row 21: K7, yo, sl1, k2tog, psso, yo.
Row 22: P10.

Row 23: K2tog, yo, k3, yo, ssk, k3.
Row 24: P10.
Row 25: Yo, k5, yo, ssk, k1, k2tog.
Row 26: P10.
Row 27: K7, yo, sl1, k2tog, psso, yo.
Row 28: P10.

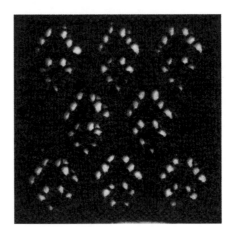

Feather and Fan

Row 1: Sl2, k2tog, p2sso, (yo, k1) x 5, yo, sl2, k2tog, p2sso, k1.
Row 2: K14.

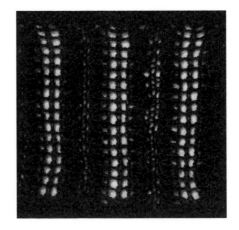

Old Shale

Row 1: K17.
Row 2: K17.
Row 3: (K2tog) x 3, (yo, k1) x 5, yo, (k2tog) x 3.
Row 4: P17.

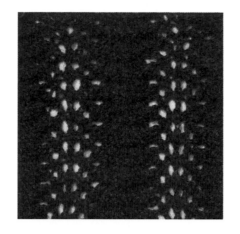

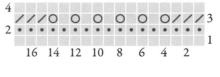

New Shale

Row 1: K1, k2tog, yo, k1, yo, k3, sl2, k1, p2sso, k3, yo, k1, yo, ssk, k1.
Row 2: P17.

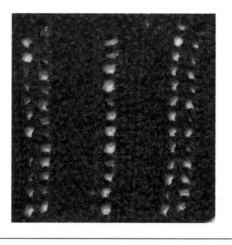

Ostrich Plumes

Row 1 (WS): P17.
Row 2: K17.
Row 3: P17.
Row 4: K1, * (yo, k1) x 2, yo, (ssk) x 2, sl2, k1, p2sso, (k2tog) x 2, (yo, k1) x 3. Rep from *.
Row 5: P17.
Row 6: K17.
Row 7: P17.
Row 8: K1, * (yo, k1) x 2, yo, (ssk) x 2, sl2, k1, p2sso, (k2tog) x 2, (yo, k1) x 3. Rep from *.
Row 9: P17.
Row 10: K17.
Row 11: P17.
Row 12: K1, * (yo, k1) x 2, yo, (ssk) x 2, sl2, k1, p2sso, (k2tog) x 2, (yo, k1) x 3. Rep from *.
Row 13: P17.
Row 14: K17.
Row 15: P17.
Row 16: K1, * (yo, k1) x 2, yo, (ssk) x 2, sl2, k1, p2sso, (k2tog) x 2, (yo, k1) x 3. Rep from *.
Row 17: P17.
Row 18: K17.
Row 19: P17.
Row 20: * (K2tog) x 2, (yo, k1) x 5, yo, (ssk) x 2, sl2, k1, p2sso. Rep from *.
Row 21: P17.
Row 22: K17.

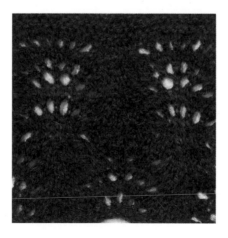

Row 23: P17.
Row 24: * (K2tog) x 2, (yo, k1) x 5, yo, (ssk) x 2, sl2, k1, p2sso. Rep from *.
Row 25: P17.
Row 26: K17.
Row 27: P17.
Row 28: * (K2tog) x 2, (yo, k1) x 5, yo, (ssk) x 2, sl2, k1, p2sso. Rep from *.
Row 29: P17.
Row 30: K17.
Row 31: P17.
Row 32: * (K2tog) x 2, (yo, k1) x 5, yo, (ssk) x 2, sl2, k1, p2sso. Rep from *.

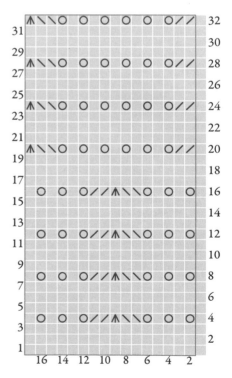

Fishtail

Row 1: Yo, k3, sl1, k2tog, psso, k3, yo, k1.
Row 2: P10.
Row 3: K1, yo, k2, sl1, k2tog, psso, k2, yo, k2.
Row 4: P10.
Row 5: K2, yo, k1, sl1, k2tog, psso, k1, yo, k3.
Row 6: P10.
Row 7: K3, yo, sl1, k2tog, psso, yo, k4.
Row 8: P10.

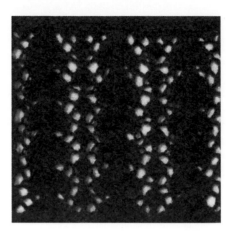

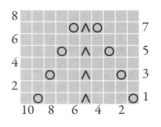

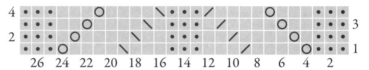

Twin Leaves

Row 1: P3, yo, k4, k2tog, k3, p3, k3, ssk, k4, yo, p3.
Row 2: K3, p1, yo, p4, p2tog tbl, p2, k3, p2, p2tog, p4, yo, p1, k3.

Row 3: P3, k2, yo, k4, k2tog, k1, p3, k1, ssk, k4, yo, k2, p3.
Row 4: K3, p3, yo, p4, p2tog tbl, k3, p2tog, p4, yo, p3, k3.

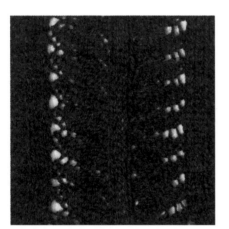

Print o' the Wave

Row 1: Yo, k2tog, k2, yo, k2, ssk, k3, k2tog, k2, yo, k2tog.
Row 2: P16.
Row 3: K2tog, yo, k3, yo, k2, ssk, k1, k2tog, k2, yo, k2tog, yo.
Row 4: P16.
Row 5: Yo, k5, yo, k2, sl1, k2tog, psso, k2, (yo, k2tog) x 2.
Row 6: P16.
Row 7: Ssk, yo, k2, ssk, k3, k2tog, k2, yo, k1, yo, ssk, yo.
Row 8: P16.
Row 9: K1, ssk, yo, k2, ssk, k1, k2tog, k2, yo, k3, yo, k1.
Row 10: P16.
Row 11: K2, ssk, yo, k2, sl1, k2tog, psso, k2, yo, k5, yo.
Row 12: P16.

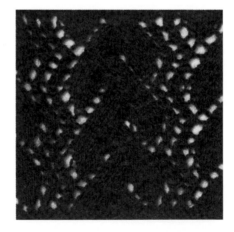

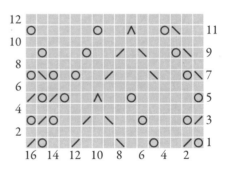

Horseshoe Lace 1

Row 1 (WS): P11.
Row 2: * K1, yo, k2tog, k5, ssk, yo.
Rep from *, k1.
Row 3: P11.
Row 4: * K1, yo, k2tog, k5, ssk, yo.
Rep from *, k1.
Row 5: P11.
Row 6: * K1, yo, k3, sl1, k2tog, psso, k3, yo.
Rep from *, k1.
Row 7: P11.
Row 8: * K2, yo, k2, sl1, k2tog, psso, k2, yo,
k1. Rep from *, k1.
Row 9: P11.
Row 10: * K3, yo, k1, sl1, k2tog, psso, k1, yo,
k2. Rep from *, k1.
Row 11: P11.
Row 12: * K4, yo, sl1, k2tog, psso, yo, k3.
Rep from *, k1.

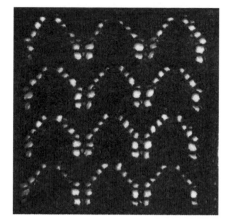

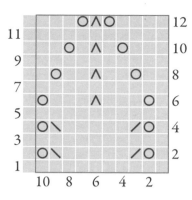

Horseshoe Lace 2

Row 1 (WS): P13.
Row 2: K1, yo, k4, sl1, k2tog, psso, k4, yo, k1.
Row 3: P13.
Row 4: K2, yo, k3, sl1, k2tog, psso, k3, yo, k2.
Row 5: P13.
Row 6: K3, yo, k2, sl1, k2tog, psso, k2, yo, k3.
Row 7: P13.
Row 8: K4, yo, k1, sl1, k2tog, psso, k1, yo, k4.
Row 9: P13.
Row 10: K5, yo, sl1, k2tog, psso, yo, k5.

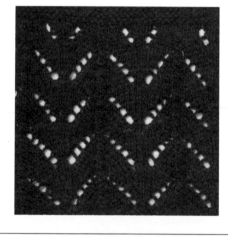

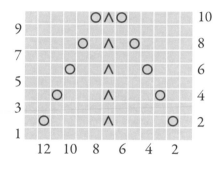

Fountain Lace

Row 1 (WS): P17.
Row 2: Ssk, yo, k2, k2tog, yo, k1, yo, sl1,
k2tog, psso, yo, k1, yo, ssk, k2, yo, k2tog.
Row 3: P17.
Row 4: Ssk, k3, yo, k2tog, yo, k3, yo, ssk,
yo, k3, k2tog.
Row 5: P17.
Row 6: Ssk, (k2, yo) x 2, k2tog, k1, ssk,
(yo, k2) x 2, k2tog.
Row 7: P17.
Row 8: Ssk, k1, yo, k3, yo, k2tog, k1, ssk,
yo, k3, yo, k1, k2tog.

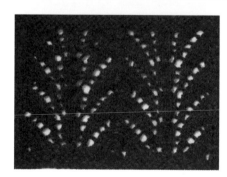

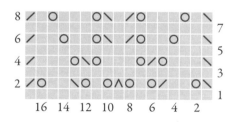

Spanish Lace

Row 1: K20.
Row 2: K20.
Row 3: Sl1, k2tog, psso, k8, yo, k1, yo, k8.
Row 4: K20.
Row 5: Sl1, k2tog, psso, k7, yo, k3, yo, k7.
Row 6: K20.
Row 7: Sl1, k2tog, psso, k6, yo, k1, yo, sl1, k2tog, psso, yo, k1, yo, k6.
Row 8: K20.
Row 9: Sl1, k2tog, psso, k5, yo, k7, yo, k5.
Row 10: K20.
Row 11: Sl1, k2tog, psso, k4, (yo, k1, yo, sl1, k2tog, psso) x 2, yo, k1, yo, k4.
Row 12: K20.
Row 13: Sl1, k2tog, psso, k3, yo, k11, yo, k3.
Row 14: K20.
Row 15: Sl1, k2tog, psso, k2, (yo, k1, yo, sl1, k2tog, psso) x 3, yo, k1, yo, k2.
Row 16: K20.

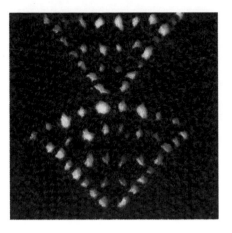

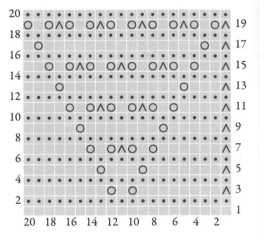

Row 17: Sl1, k2tog, psso, k1, yo, k15, yo, k1.
Row 18: K20.
Row 19: (Sl1, k2tog, psso, yo, k1, yo) x 5.
Row 20: K20.

Queen's Lace

Row 1: K1, yo, k2tog, k3, (k2tog, yo) x 2, ssk, yo, k1, yo, k2tog, (yo, ssk) x 2, k3, ssk, yo, k1.
Row 2: P5, p2tog tbl, yo, p11, yo, p2tog, p5.
Row 3: K1, yo, k2tog, (k1, k2tog, yo) x 2, k1, ssk, yo, k1, yo, k2tog, (k1, yo, ssk) x 2, k1, ssk, yo, k1.
Row 4: P3, p2tog tbl, yo, p15, yo, p2tog, p3.
Row 5: (K2, k2tog, yo) x 2, k2, ssk, yo, k1, yo, k2tog, (k2, yo, ssk) x 2, k2.
Row 6: P1, p2tog tbl, yo, p19, yo, p2tog, p1.
Row 7: (K2tog, yo, k3) x 2, ssk, yo, k1, yo, k2tog, (k3, yo, ssk) x 2.
Row 8: P25.
Row 9: K1, yo, k2tog, (yo, ssk) x 2, k3, ssk, yo, k1, yo, k2tog, k3, (k2tog, yo) x 2, ssk, yo, k1.
Row 10: P6, yo, p2tog, p9, p2tog tbl, yo, p6.
Row 11: K1, yo, k2tog, (k1, yo, ssk) x 2, k1, ssk, yo, k1, yo, k2tog, (k1, k2tog, yo) x 2, k1, ssk, yo, k1.
Row 12: P8, yo, p2tog, p5, p2tog tbl, yo, p8.
Row 13: K1, yo, k2tog, (k2, yo, ssk) x 2, k3, (k2tog, yo, k2) x 2, ssk, yo, k1.

Row 14: P10, yo, p2tog, p1, p2tog tbl, yo, p10.
Row 15: K1, yo, k2tog, k3, yo, ssk, k3, yo, sl1, k2tog, psso, yo, k3, k2tog, yo, k3, ssk, yo, k1.
Row 16: P25.

Wings of a Swan

Row 1 (WS): P23.
Row 2: K4, (k2tog, yo) x 2, k1, yo, ssk, k1, k2tog, yo, k1, (yo, ssk) x 2, k4.
Row 3: P23.
Row 4: K3, (k2tog, yo) x 2, k1, yo, ssk, yo, sl1, k2tog, psso, yo, k2tog, yo, k1, (yo, ssk) x 2, k3.
Row 5: P23.
Row 6: K2, (k2tog, yo) x 2, k1, (yo, ssk) x 2, k1, (k2tog, yo) x 2, k1, (yo, ssk) x 2, k2.
Row 7: P23.
Row 8: K1, (k2tog, yo) x 2, k3, yo, ssk, yo, sl1, k2tog, psso, yo, k2tog, yo, k3, (yo, k2tog) x 2, k1.
Row 9: P23.
Row 10: (K1, (yo, ssk) x 2, k2, (k2tog, yo) x 2) x 2, k1.
Row 11: P23.
Row 12: K2, (yo, ssk) x 2, (k2tog, yo) x 2, k3,

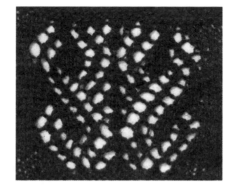

(yo, ssk) x 2, (k2tog, yo) x 2, k2.
Row 13: P23.
Row 14: K3, yo, ssk, (k2tog, yo) x 2, k1, yo, sl1, k2tog, psso, yo, k1, (yo, ssk) x 2, k2tog, yo, k3.

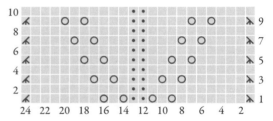

Fern Lace

Row 1: K3tog tbl, k7, yo, k, yo, p2, yo, k, yo, k7, k3tog.
Row 2: P11, k2, p11.
Row 3: K3tog tbl, k6, (yo, k) x 2, p2, (k, yo) x 2, k6, k3tog.
Row 4: P11, k2, p11.
Row 5: K3tog tbl, k5, yo, k, yo, k2, p2, k2, yo, k, yo, k5, k3tog.
Row 6: P11, k2, p11.
Row 7: K3tog tbl, k4, yo, k, yo, k3, p2, k3, yo, k, yo, k4, k3tog.
Row 8: P11, k2, p11.
Row 9: K3tog tbl, k3, yo, k, yo, k4, p2, k4, yo, k, yo, k3, k3tog.
Row 10: P11, k2, p11.

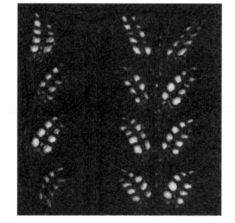

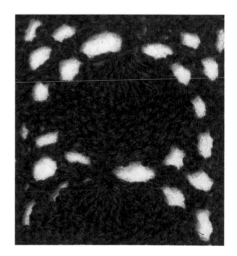

Cockleshell

Row 1: K19.
Row 2: K19.
Row 3: K1, (yo) x 2, p2tog, k13, p2tog, (yo) x 2, k1.
Row 4: K2, p1, k15, p1, k2.
Row 5: K25.
Row 6: K25.
Row 7: K1, ((yo) x 2, p2tog) x 2, k11, (p2tog, (yo) x 2) x 2, k1.
Row 8: (K2, p1) x 2, k13, (p1, k2) x 2.
Row 9: K25.
Row 10: K6, ((yo) x 2, k1) x 13, (yo) x 2, k6.
Row 11: (K1, (yo) x 2) x 3, p15tog, ((yo) x 2, k1) x 3.
Row 12: K1, (p1, k2) x 2, p1, k3, (p1, k2) x 2, p1, k1.

Lacy Socks

Lace patterns can be loose and open or, when the yarn overs are combined with purl stitches, produce interesting rib sections that give the lace a degree of stretch. Here, a very simple eyelet rib lace stitch has been used to give these summer socks their ribbed texture, while a horseshoe lace stitch has been added afterwards to give the cuff of each sock a more delicate finish.

Size
The socks will fit a small (medium, large)

Materials
1 (2, 2) x 1¾oz (50g) balls pale turquoise
sport-weight yarn
Size 3 (5, 6)/3.25 (3.75, 4) mm double-
pointed needles

Gauge
Not important for this project if you use
a stretchy rib

ABOVE: *Detail of the ribbed section that
provides some elasticity over the foot.*

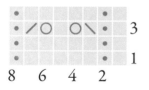

Cast on 56 sts and divide between three
needles, being careful not to twist sts.
Work 10 rounds k1, p1 rib.
Work 1 round purl.
Work 1 round plain.
Now work four rows of pattern.
Round 1: *K1, p1, k5, p1. Rep from * to end.
Round 2: Rep Round 1.
Round 3: *K1, p1, ssk, yo, k1, yo, k2tog. Rep
from * to end.
Round 4: Rep Round 1.
Continue in pattern until leg measures 4
(4¾, 5½) in/10 (12, 14) cm, slip first and
last sets of 14 sts onto one needle and leave
rem 28 sts for instep.

SHAPE HEEL
Row 1: Sl1, k to last st, turn.
Row 2: Sl1, p to last st, turn.
Row 3: Sl1, k to last 2 sts, turn.
Row 4: P to last 2 sts, turn.
Cont working 1 less st each row until the row
sl1, k to last 8, has been worked.
Next row: Sl1, p to last 8, turn.
Next row: Sl1, k to last 7, turn.
Next row: Sl1, p to last 7, turn.
Cont in this way, working 1 more stitch on
every row until all 28 sts are back on needle.

Divide the sts onto three needles again and
continue with eyelet pattern over 25 sts on
instep and the rem in st st.
When foot measures 5 (6, 6¾) in/13
(15, 17) cm, work 2 rounds of knit placing
sts 14, 28, 14 on needles.

SHAPE TOE
Needle 1: K to last 3, k2tog, k1.
Needle 2: K1, ssk, k to last 3, k2tog, k1,
Needle 3: K1, ssk, k to end.
Knit next round.
Rep from * ending these 2 rounds to
22 (24, 24) sts.
Graft sts together, or bind off together
on inside.

CUFF
With right side facing, pick up 56 sts from
ridges formed by purl round below ribbing.
Knit 1 more round increasing evenly to 60 sts.

Work horseshoe lace, or similar lace pattern
of your choice, increasing to the number of
stitches required as appropriate.
Round 1: * K1 , yo, k2tog, k5, ssk, yo.
Rep from *.
Round 2 and all alt rows: K.
Round 3: * K1 yo, k2tog, k5, ssk, yo.
Rep from *.
Round 5: * K1, yo, k3, s1k2togpsso, k3, yo.
Rep from *.
Round 7: * K2 yo, k2, s1k2togpsso, k2, yo,
k1. Rep from *.
Round 9: * K3 yo, k1, s1k2togpsso, k1, yo,
k2. Rep from *.
Round 11: * K4 yo, s1k2togpsso, yo, k3.
Rep from *.
Work 3 rounds garter st and bind off.
Weave in any loose ends.

ALTERNATIVE STITCHES
*The eyelet rib pattern here could be swapped
for ribbed lace or cat's face rib, both on page
92. In each case, remember that you would
have an extra knit stitch at the beginning
and end of the round.*

*When it comes to the lace frill you can
be as adventurous as you want. Pick up the
stitches from around the top rib and then
increase them to give a fuller frill and choose
any of the lace patterns that will fit nicely
over between 12 and 20 rows. Examples
include falling leaves on page 96, feather and
fan on page 98, twin leaves on page 100, and
old shale on page 99. They would all give a
nice scalloped edge at the finish.*

Hap Shawl

The Shetland hap shawl was once the most popular item of knitwear on the Scottish islands and the mainland. It was worn by the women themselves, as well as being made for sale. The shawl pattern shown here is typical of those worn folded into a triangle and crossed at the front. If they were long enough, they could be tied at the back, otherwise they would be tucked into the belt or pinned where they crossed. Sometimes the center would be worked in stockinette stitch, but more often it was garter stitch. The old shale stitch was the one most frequently used for the borders, often with bands of natural colors of Shetland wool.

Size

The shawl measures approximately 50 x 50in (125 x 125cm)

Materials

10½oz (300g) yarn in total:
1 x 1¾oz (50g) ball cream sport-weight yarn
1 x 1¾oz (50g) ball plum sport-weight yarn
1 x 1¾oz (50g) ball dark-pink sport-weight yarn
1 x 1¾oz (50g) ball brown sport-weight yarn
1 x 1¾oz (50g) ball fawn sport-weight yarn
1 x 1¾oz (50g) ball mushroom sport-weight yarn
Size 8 (5mm) straight needles

Gauge

18 sts and 21 rows – 4in (10cm)

Chart for edging

CENTER

Using cream, cast on 3sts.
Row 1: Yo, k to end.
Row 2: Yo, p to end.
Repeat these two rows until there are 48 loops at each side.

Decrease at each end of every row as follows:
Row 1: Yo, k3tog, k to end.
Row 2: Yo, p3tog, p to end.
Repeat these two rows until there are 3sts. K3tog, but do not break off yarn.

Continuing with cream, pick up and knit 48 loops along one side.
Knit 1 more row.
Set pattern:
Row 1: Yo, k3, *(yo, k1) x 6, k6. Rep from * ending (yo, k1) x 6, k3.
Row 2: Yo, k to end.
Rows 3 & 4: Rep Row 2.

Change to plum and begin old shale pattern
Row 5: Yo, k2, (k2tog) x 3 * (yo, k1) x 6, (k2tog) x 6. Rep from * ending (k2tog) x 3, k2.
Rows 6, 7 & 8: Rep Row 2.
Row 9: Yo, k3, k2tog, yo, k1, (k2tog) x 2, * (yo, k1) x 6, (k2tog) x 6. Rep from * ending (k2tog) x 2, k1, yo, k2tog, k3.
Rows 10, 11 & 12: Rep Row 2.
Row 13: Yo, k3, (yo, k1) x 2, (k2tog) x 4, * (yo, k1) x 6, (k2tog) x 6. Rep from * ending (k2tog) x 4, (yo, k1) x 2, k3.
Rows 14, 15 & 16: Rep Row 2.

Change to fawn
Row 17: Yo, k3 (yo, k1) x 3, (k2tog) x 5, * (yo, k1) x 6, (k2tog) x 6. Rep from * ending (k2tog) x 5, (yo, k1) x 3, k3.
Rows 18, 19 & 20: Rep Row 2.
Row 21: Yo, k3 (yo, k1) x 4, (k2tog) x 6, * (yo, k1) x 6, (k2tog) x 6. Rep from * ending (yo, k1) x 4, k3.

Rows 22, 23 & 24: P as Row 2.
Row 25: Yo, k3, k2tog, (yo, k1) x 5, (k2tog) x 6, *(yo, k1) x 6, (k2tog) x 6. Rep from * ending (yo, k1) x 5, k2tog, k3.
Rows 26, 27 & 28: Rep Row 2.

Change to dark pink
Row 29: Yo, k3, (k2tog) x 2, * (yo, k1) x 6, (k2tog) x 6. Rep from * ending (yo, k1) x 6, (k2tog) x 2, k3.
Rows 30, 31 & 32: Rep Row 2.
Row 33: Yo, k3, yo, k1, (k2tog) x 3, * (yo, k1) x 6, (k2tog) x 6. Rep from * ending (k2tog) x 3, k1, yo, k3.
Rows 34, 35 & 36: Rep Row 2.
Row 37: Yo, k3 (yo, k1) x 2, (k2tog) x 4, * (yo, k1) x 6, (k2tog) x 6. Rep from * ending (k2tog) x 4, (yo, k1) x 2, k3.
Rows 38, 39 & 40: P as Row 2.
Row 41: Yo, k3 (yo, k1) x 3, (k2tog) x 5, * yo, k1) x 6, (k2tog) x 6. Rep from * ending (k2tog) x 5, (yo, k1) x 3, k3.
Rows 42, 43 & 44: Rep Row 2.

Change to brown
Row 45: Yo, k3 (yo, k1) x 4, (k2tog) x 6, * (yo, k1) x 6, (k2tog) x 6. Rep from * ending (yo, k1) x 4, k3.
Rows 46, 47 & 48: Rep Row 2.
Row 49: Yo, k3, k2tog (yo, k1) x 5, (k2tog) x 6, * (yo, k1) x 6, (k2tog) x 6. Rep from * ending (yo, k1) x 5, k2tog, k3.
Rows 50, 51 & 52: Rep Row 2.

Row 53: Yo, k3, (k2tog) x 2, * (yo, k1) x 6, (k2tog) x 6. Rep from * ending (yo, k1) x 6, (k2tog) x 2, k3.
Rows 54, 55 & 56: Rep Row 2.
Row 57: Yo, k3, yo, k1, (k2tog) x 3, * (yo, k1) x 6, (k2tog) x 6. Rep from * ending (k2tog) x 3, k1, yo, k3.
Rows 58, 59, & 60: Rep Row 2. Leave sts on needle.

Change to mushroom
Cast on 11 sts for edging. K10, k2tog (the last stitch of the edging together with the 1st of the sts on the needle). Work from chart or instructions, knitting the last st together with the next on the needle each time.

HAP SHAWL EDGING
Row 1: K3, yo, ssk, k2, yo, ssk, yo, k2.
Row 2: K11, k2tog.
Row 3: K2, (yo, ssk) x 2, k2, yo, ssk, yo, k2.
Row 4: K12, k2tog.
Row 5: K3, (yo, ssk) x 2, k2, yo, ssk, yo, k2.
Row 6: K13, k2tog.
Row 7: K2, (yo, ssk) x 3, k2, yo, ssk, yo, k2.
Row 8: K14, k2tog.
Row 9: (K2, (k2tog, yo) x 2) x 2, k2tog, k1.
Row 10: K13, k2tog.
Row 11: K1, k2tog, yo, k2tog, k3, (k2tog, yo) x 2, k2tog, k1.
Row 12: K12, k2tog.
Row 13: (K2, k2tog, yo) x 2, k2tog, yo, k2tog, k1.

Row 14: K11, k2tog.
Row 15: K1, k2tog, yo, k2, (k2tog, yo) x 2, k2tog, k1.
Row 16: P2tog, k9, k2tog.
When all of the first border stitches have been knitted together leave stitches from edging on holder and work each of following three borders to match.

FINISHING
When the four sides are completed, join the sides of each border with a loose herringbone stitch, matching the colors. Join the cast-on and bind-off edges of the border together. Block the shawl by wrapping it in a damp towel overnight, then spread it out flat, pinning the corners square. Leave it to dry naturally.

ALTERNATIVE STITCHES
You could replace the old shale stitch with the feather and fan on page 98 or a similar pattern to the eyelet rib used for the socks on page 105. The borders can be made as deep as you choose. Once they are finished, you could add a lace edging as we have done here.

Chapter Six
COLORWORK

In use for many centuries, colorwork knitting
techniques have a diverse history and range from
elaborate religious pieces worked in minute silk
stitches to rough-and-ready raw-wool garments
designed for braving the elements out of doors. Time
and again, the appeal of such pieces lies in the impact
of the patterns achieved. Whether the focus is a simple
repeating pattern of geometric blocks or a single
striking motif, such as a star, animal, or snowflake,
each is achievable in an infinite variety of colorways.

Patterns and Motifs

For impoverished inhabitants of cold regions, working with scraps of yarn in two or more colors was economical and, because of the way in which pieces were knit, produced warm, durable clothing. These two factors have contributed many beautiful patterns over the years.

Color-knitting traditions go back many thousands of years. In fact, the earliest piece of knitting that appears to have been made with two hand-held needles was found in Egypt and dates from 1000 CE. It is a pair of socks, elaborately patterned and worked in fine cotton yarn in blue and white.

Traditionally knitting fibers were colored using local indigenous dyes. Cotton, flax, wool, and silk were the most usual fibers in the beginning. All of them took well to dyes, derived from plants including logwood, madder root, and saffron, or animal dyes such as

cochineal, extracted from insects. In the case of the Egyptian socks, the blue was obtained from woad, *isatis tinctoria*, a widespread plant that produces a range of blues. The most common dyeing technique was to immerse the spun wool in a boiling solution of the dye, often resulting in strong and vibrant colors.

Early Colorwork

Some of the earliest surviving examples of intricate European colorwork can be found in Spain, and include cushions and gloves found in the tomb of Prince Fernando de la Cerda, who died in 1275.

ABOVE: *Wools that have been colored using natural dyes have always been popular. Source materials and dyeing methods remain largely unchanged for many centuries.*

Among them, a silk cushion cover was knit at approximately 20 stitches to the inch and included heraldic devices as well as lettering in Arabic. Numerous other knitted items from the 13th century, featuring complex colorwork patterns usually of a religious or geometric nature, have also been found in cathedral treasuries. A later pair of Spanish liturgical gloves has a motif on

ABOVE: *The Norwegian star pattern on these gloves became a popular Fair Isle motif following the Second World War, when many Norwegians came to Shetland as refugees.*

LEFT: *An elderly Cowichan lady on Vancouver Island in British Columbia knits a distinctively patterned, heavy-knit* siwash *sweater, traditionally made using a combination of knitting and weaving skills.*

the wrist section similar to that of the Islamic Pattern on page 126.

Elsewhere, relic purses from Switzerland, used for holding the bones of saints were also knitted in natural colors, with madder or indigo used as the dyes. A purse found in Chur, Switzerland, has similar heraldic motifs to those found on the Spanish cushion cover, while another one in blue and white has a motif not unlike that of the Finnish Border 1 swatch on page 117.

The Americas

The Spanish introduced knitting to the Americas as early as the 16th century, with their colonization of South America. The tradition is still extremely popular there today, especially in Peru and Bolivia, where brightly colored shawls and caps with earflaps are a familiar sight. Traditionally, men did the knitting, while the women spun the wool, but now both men and women knit. They have an unusual style, in that the yarn passes around the back of the neck and down the left hand, where it is picked up by the needle in the manner of Continental knitting.

From the 19th century onwards, European settlers were once again to influence knitting trends in the Americas, this time the Cowichan people of British Columbia. Among the techniques they passed on were knitting in the round and color-stranding. From the 20th century to this day, the Cowichan have combined the two to make clothing—typically socks, mittens and sweaters—using raw wool in shades from cream to dark brown, the natural fleece colors of their mountain sheep. Similar to the color-stranding techniques more readily associated with their Nordic settlers, Cowichan sweater designs are often referred to as *siwash* (a term that derives from the French *sauvage*, meaning "wild") and include a large central pictorial motif—an eagle, bear, or a moose, for example—with horizontal bands of patterning above and below and on the sleeves.

Nordic Traditions

The color-stranding technique adopted by the Cowichan people is thought to have been introduced by northern Europeans around 1900, and involves knitting with two or more strands of yarn at a time. Although the technique

RIGHT: *The circular band of pattern at the yoke is a typical feature of the Icelandic* lopi *sweater. Knitted in the round, there is no difference between the front and the back.*

is used to produce beautiful patterned pieces, it first came into being for practical reasons. Any garment knitted with two strands of wool will be doubly thick, and therefore extra warm. Initially, garments were knitted with woolen-spun yarn (that is yarn that has been spun from fleece that has been carded only; worsted yarn is spun from fleece that has been carded and combed), which has a greater tendency to felt than worsted yarn. This means that, after washing, color-stranded knitting would become a denser and even warmer fabric. It is for this reason that the technique is most associated with countries in the northern latitudes—Sweden, Norway, Finland, Scotland, Iceland, and the Faroe Islands.

In Iceland, hand-knitting dates back to the early 1700s. Traditional garments were knitted in two, sometimes three different colors. The patterns created were subtle, since only natural wool colors were used and designs were made up of small, interlocking squares and diamonds. The wool used for knitting came from Icelandic sheep, a breed introduced into the island by the Vikings in the 9th century CE. This primitive breed has a dual coat; it has a long-haired, protective outer coat, and a soft, short-haired, insulating inner coat. This fluffy inner wool traps pockets of air, and so this part of the fleece was spun into a thick yarn that was ideal for creating warm sweaters. Color-stranding techniques combined with felting meant that sweaters were ideally suited for the harsh North Atlantic climate.

Traditionally, Scandinavian countries preferred two-stranded knitting, either in color or as a textured pattern, both of which made the item warmer because of the double layer. Among the most popular motifs still used today are the eight-pointed star, also known as the Norwegian Star (see page 118), or Selburose, which apparently originated in Selbu in the 19th century, when a young local, Marit Ermstad chose to knit a pair of mittens featuring a design she

had copied from a piece of embroidery. A pattern for a modern version of these mittens is given in the project section. The original was knitted in black and white, as was the tradition in Norway, evidenced by the *luskofte*—black-and-white speckled jerseys with yokes patterned with a wide range of motifs influenced by Scandinavian flora and fauna—birds, flowers, and reindeer.

Scottish knitters created two distinct forms of colorwork of their own, notably Argyle patterns and Sanquhar patterns (see page 120). These patterns may have derived from the type of local woven cloths of checks and plaids that prevailed. It is just as likely that they came about naturally because of the way stitches obviously lend themselves to geometric forms.

Fair Isle Knitting

Although the term "Fair Isle" is often applied to any knitting featuring multiple patterns and colors, it is actually more specific than that and should only be applied to the unique style of knitting from the island of that name, which lies between the Orkney and Shetland Islands, off the coast of Scotland. Many

of the traditional patterns have crossed boundaries, however—especially those between Scandinavia and Shetland—and are now more widespread.

Limited supplies of materials found on the islands determined that knitters would make the most of the wool they had; working bands of different patterns is a more effective way of using small amounts of color. Although patterns are made up of several colors, only two are used in each round of the design. By subtly shifting the combinations of color in both the background and in the motif, the designs appear more complex than those of other color-stranded traditions. Skillful knitters prided themselves on never repeating the same pattern in the body of a garment. It is not difficult to devise a logical and balanced pattern with, say, five stitches between color changes, as can be seen from many of the patterns in this chapter.

Historically, Fair Isle knitting was carried out using three long, fine, steel, double-pointed needles, known as "wires." Knitters divided their garment stitches between two needles and then used the third "free" needle to work them. The non-working ends of the first

LEFT: *In this 1930s photograph, taken at Busta on Fair Isle, Tomima Stout is seen wearing a makkin belt and using the three-needle method to knit a sweater.*

BELOW: *Johnnie Jamieson of Unst, in Shetland, sits by the fireside wearing an allover Fair Isle sweater and a tam o'shanter in this mid-20th-century photograph.*

two needles were then held steady in a knitting sheath, worn on a belt, while the knitting was in progress. An alternative to the sheath was the makkin belt; this leather belt, worn round the waist, featured an enlarged and padded section, pierced with holes into which the needle tips were slotted.

Most of the traditional Fair Isle and Shetland patterns were based around the symmetrical pattern known as OXO (see page 122), because of the pattern's resemblance to those letters. While each of the motifs may have a different design, the outer edge always resembles this OXO shape. Examples of this include the cap pattern (see page 123) and the flower border (see page 124). This last is

the variation that has been used for the child's Fair Isle sweater that follows the stitch directory (see pages 127–129).

The first historic evidence of Fair Isle knitting is a description of a multicolored cap found in a book of 1822 about the Shetland Islands. No large examples exist from before the early 20th century; since such knitwear was designed for everyday wear rather than being set aside for special occasions, this is hardly surprising. Until it became fashionable, Fair Isle knitwear was purely practical, and was worn until it wore out.

Printed patterns for Fair Isle designs did not appear in books or magazines until the 1920s. Up until that point, knitters kept their own record of

patterns in personal notebooks or in knitted samples. Some knew designs that had been passed down through the generations. While traditional patterns and motifs were maintained and remained popular, Fair Isle knitters frequently adapted and altered them to create a range of different designs.

In the 1920s, the Fair Isle knit became a fashion item. Edward, Prince of Wales (later Edward VIII), was given a Fair Isle sweater by the Shetland draper James Smith in 1922. He wore the pullover while playing golf at St Andrews and later had his portrait painted wearing it. In an era when casual clothing and sportswear were being popularized, the Fair Isle sweater was the ideal garment.

Colorwork Stitches

The majority of colorwork patterns are represented in chart form, rather than as written instructions, where one square on a chart equals one stitch of knitting. If knitting on two needles, the right-side rows are read from right to left and wrong side rows from left to right. If knitting in the round, all rows are read from right to left. Be consistent with the way you hold the yarns—for example, always hold the main color in your normal way and the contrast color either in your left hand or over your right middle finger. This will show the pattern to best advantage. As you knit, pull the stitches back along the right needle in order to prevent puckering.

Brick Stitch
Change colors every two rows as on chart.
Row 1: K19.
Row 2: P19.
Row 3: K1, (sl, k3) x 4, sl, k1.
Row 4: P1, (sl wyif, p3) x 4, sl wyif, p1.
Row 5: K19.
Row 6: p19.
Row 7: (K3, sl) x 4, k3.
Row 8: (P3, sl wyif) x 4, p3.
Row 9: K19.
Row 10: P19.
Row 11: K1, (sl, k3) x 4, sl, k1.
Row 12: P1, (sl wyif, p3) x 4, sl wyif, p1.
Row 13: K19.
Row 14: P19.
Row 15: (K3, sl) x 4, k3.

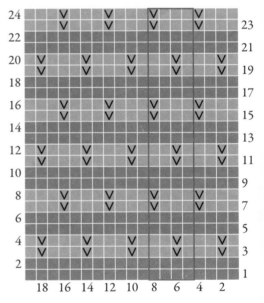

Row 16: (P3, sl wyif) x 4, p3.
Row 17: K19.
Row 18: P19.
Row 19: K1, (sl, k3) x 4, sl, k1.
Row 20: P1, (sl wyif, p3) x 4, sl wyif, p1.
Row 21: K19.
Row 22: P19.
Row 23: (K3, sl) x 4, k3.
Row 24: (P3, sl wyif) x 4, p3.

■ Purple
■ Olive

Slip Stitch Check
Row 1: K1, (sl, k3) x 2, sl, k1.
Row 2: P1, (sl, p3) x 2, sl, p1.
Row 3: (K3, sl) x 2, k3.
Row 4: (P3, sl) x 2, p3.
Row 5: K1, (sl, k3) x 2, sl, k1.
Row 6: P1, (sl, p3) x 2, sl, p1.
Row 7: (K3, sl) x 2, k3.
Row 8: (P3, sl) x 2, p3.

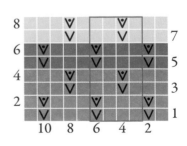

■ Fawn
■ Raspberry
■ Olive
■ Purple

Finnish Border 1

A simple, two-color border pattern in the blue and white of the Finnish flag. The small crosses top and bottom are found in Scottish and Turkish knitting, too. It is the most obvious motif for a technique based on a grid.

 Shetland

Blue

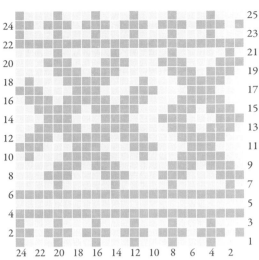

Finnish Border 2

As with the example above, this design is typically used for embellishing mittens. It is often worked in two colors rather than the four shown here. Note the use of the small crosses again, at the top and bottom.

Purple

Yellow

Lime green

Damson

Fawn

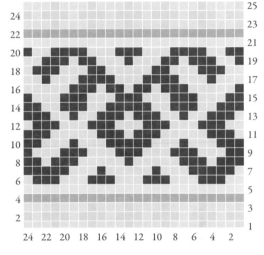

Baltic Circle

There is a crossover between this pattern and a number of the Scottish and Fair Isle examples. A border around the four diamonds would make it very similar to the central motif in the purse pattern on page 123.

 Cream

Moorit

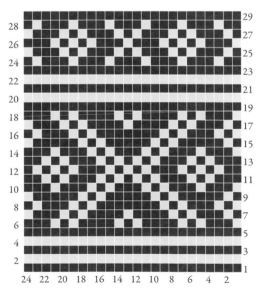

Norwegian Star

This is the large Norwegian motif that was introduced into the Shetland Islands during the Second World War. There had always been star motifs in Shetland but this one is much larger and more square shaped.

 Purple
Slate

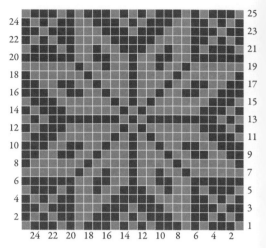

Four-color Star

This interpretation of the Norwegian star can be used as pattern band or an allover design.

Fuchsia
Slate
Purple
Sloe
Mushroom

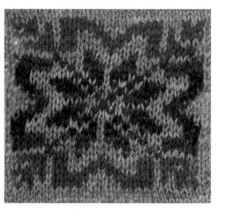

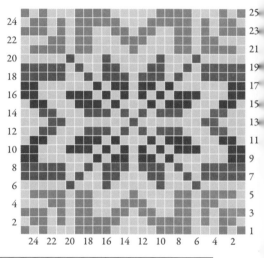

Selbu Star

This star or snowflake motif was usually worked in one color on the back of Norwegian mittens. Different knitters would devise their own or make alterations to a design they had seen elsewhere.

 Slate
Yellow
Damson
Mushroom
Purple
Olive

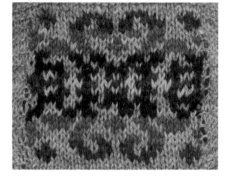

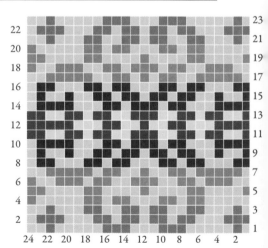

Norwegian Snowflake

The shading used here is typical of the way these motifs were worked in Shetland.

- Rasberry
- Turquoise
- Olive
- Purple
- Damson
- Sloe
- Light Brown
- Fawn
- Biscuit

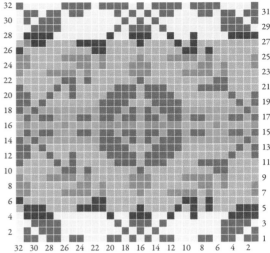

Norwegian Reindeer

The reindeer comes in many forms, and is one of several animal motifs that originated in northern Europe. Typically, two are worked facing each other across the yoke of a sweater.

- Plum
- Grey

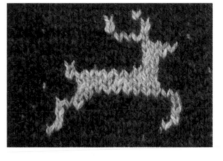

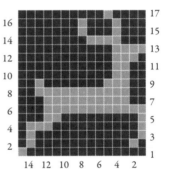

Norwegian Flower

Floral designs are a popular choice for mittens in Nordic countries. Rows 1 to 17 could be used on their own as a border pattern on a pair of socks or mittens, or around the neck or hem of a sweater.

- Light Green
- Yellow
- Cream

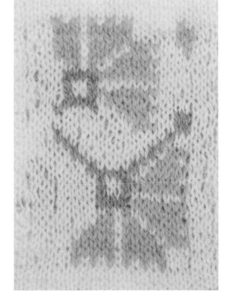

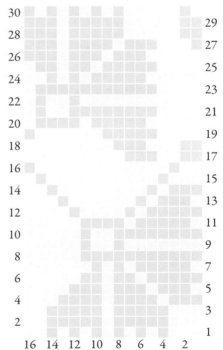

Shepherd's Plaid

Traditional Sanquhar patterns like this and the cornet and drum, below, are based on two, high-contrast colors worked in simple geometric patterns. This particular check is based on an old tartan design.

Cream

Moorit

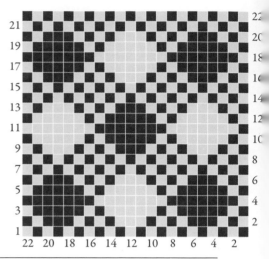

Cornet and Drum

Sanquhar patterns were traditionally used for gloves but there is no reason why they cannot be used for any knitted item. An enlarged version of this one, for example, would be ideal for a throw or a cushion.

Moorit

Mushroom

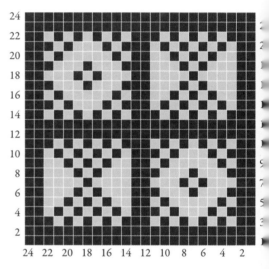

Argyle

Argyle patterns often imitated Scottish tartan patterns for kilt hose. When made in more than two colors they were knitted on two needles rather than worked in the round, in order to get the yarn in the right position.

Yellow

Damson

Saltire and Cross

Some Shetland patterns were worked all over rather than in bands, as in Fair Isle patterns. This example alternates the saltire cross of the Scottish flag set within a square background with an upright cross set within a diamond.

■ Mushroom
■ Slate

Scottish Allover Pattern

This striking example of a traditional allover pattern uses the same cross motif as the saltire and cross, above. Here, however, it set within a larger, stitched diamond border.

■ Dark Brown
■ Oxblood
■ Lime Green

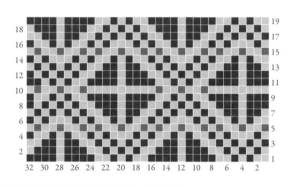

Cross Border

This is another pattern based on the cross within a diamond, worked in bands, with a simple geometric pattern to outline it.

■ Pink
■ Purple
■ Blue
■ Mushroom
■ Navy
■ Slate

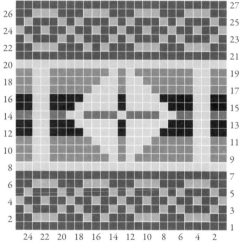

OXO Pattern

Traditional Fair Isle patterns work best in shades of the same color (or colors adjacent to one another on the color wheel) for the outer bands and 1–3 rows of a strong contrast through the center. This pattern takes its name from the letters it resembles.

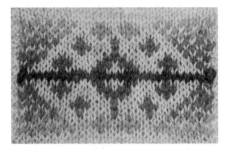

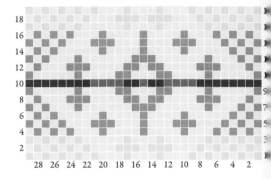

- 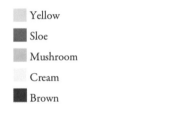 Raspberry
- Slate
- Lime Green
- Fawn
- Light Blue
- Purple

Edward VIII

This motif is based on one that was featured in a Fair Isle sweater worn by Edward VIII in the 1920s. It would work very well in combination with the OXO pattern, the purse pattern and the cap pattern.

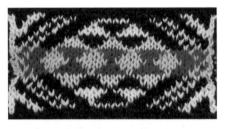

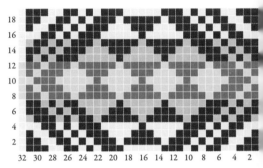

- Yellow
- Sloe
- Mushroom
- Cream
- Brown

Cross and Drum

While some Fair Isle patterns work well in larger blocks of color as here, it would be equally interesting to see them changing color every two rows on the outer portions.

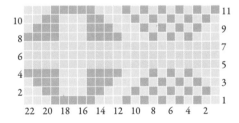

- Lime Green
- Blue
- Fawn

Small Stars

This is a traditional star design from the Shetland Islands, and was in use before the large Norwegian designs became popular. Similar stars, only nine rows high, were also used between the wider pattern bands.

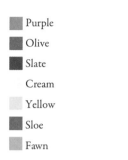 Purple

 Olive

 Slate

Cream

Yellow

 Sloe

 Fawn

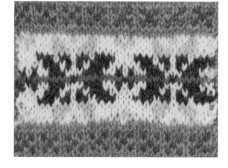

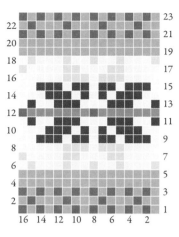

Purse Pattern

This is a typical pattern, used on early knitted stocking caps. It would have been worked mainly in red and blue, with a touch of yellow or white at that time.

 Sloe

Olive

Brown

Yellow

Mushroom

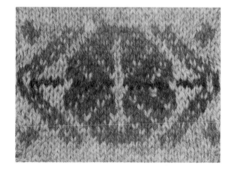

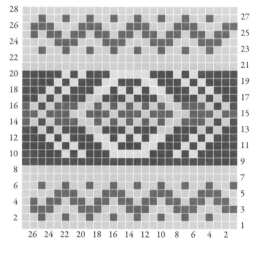

Cap Pattern

Based on the OXO motif, this pattern would traditionally have been worked in natural dyes of indigo blue, madder red, and onion skin yellow on a natural white background.

 Olive

Yellow

Sloe

Purple

Light Blue

Mushroom

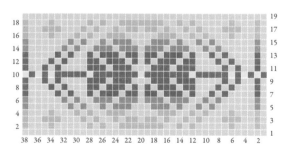

Flower Border

This flower pattern is used in the Fair Isle Sweater on pages 127–129. Look closely and you will see that the petals of the flower resemble hearts. Perhaps it was derived from the pattern in the heart border chart below.

 Purple

Olive

Mid-brown

Navy Blue

Plum

Fawn

Mid-blue

Mushroom

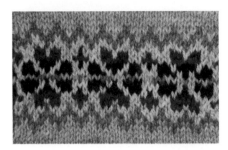

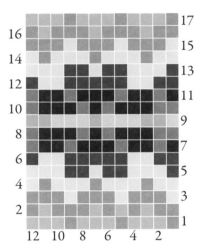

Heart Border

The geometric pattern used in this design is one that crops up in many other countries. In Scotland, small geometric patterns like this are referred to as "peeries" or "peerie patterns."

 Fawn

Purple

Pink

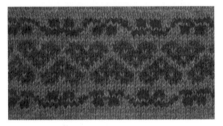

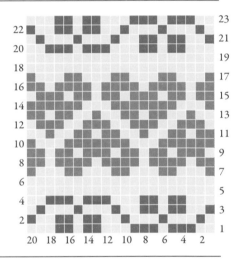

Diamonds and Hearts

Fair Isle motifs tend to have the same number of stitches as rows to the inch. You will need to remember to allow for this change in gauge if you are working plain sections between the bands of color.

 Plum

Olive

Fuchsia

Fawn

Yellow

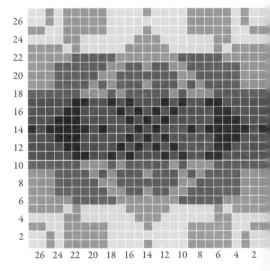

Cross and Snowflake

The appearance of a motif can alter significantly if the background color is changed as well as the motif color. If this one's background were worked entirely in cream it would look very different.

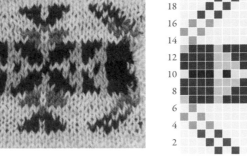

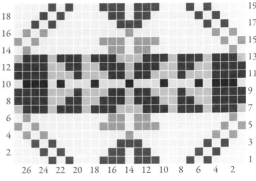

■ Damson

Yellow

■ Lime green

■ Light blue

Fawn

■ Brown

Snowflake

Try working this motif with a more frequent change of colors—for example, with the middle band in two contrasting colors. Shade colors gradually from light to dark, then work them in reverse for a different look.

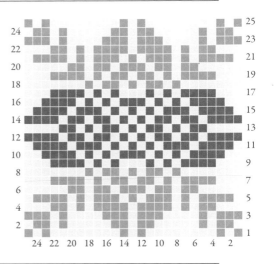

■ Indigo

Cream

■ Pink

Tree of Life

This motif is seen in various textile traditions. There are similarities between this design and the textured version on page 22. If you omit Rows 1 to 6 on the chart, you can use the design as a repeating, allover pattern.

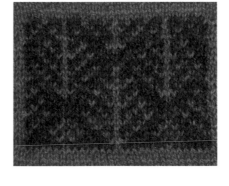

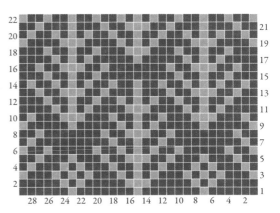

■ Blue

■ Slate

125

Islamic Pattern

Scrolling, interlacing patterns like this are associated with designs from the Middle East, and are inspired by Arabic art and calligraphy. This Islamic pattern would make an interesting border on a jacket or bag.

▢ Blue

▢ Cream

■ Slate

Eastern European Pattern

Reminiscent of the Greek key design, this motif makes a striking repeating pattern and would work especially well done in the round. Strong contrasting colors show it to the greatest advantage.

■ Brown

▢ Cream

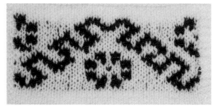

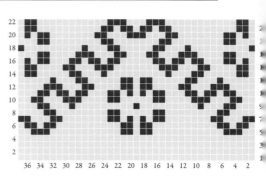

Turkish Sock Pattern

This pattern was originally used for knitting socks from the toe up and worked in bands of different colors. It is just as interesting worked in two colors and would make an unusual allover pattern for a bag or a cushion.

■ Purple

▢ Lime Green

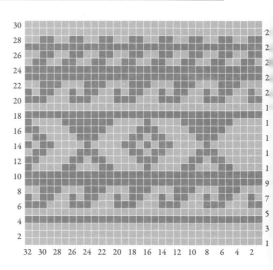

Fair Isle Sweater

Fair Isle patterns may look complicated, but once you get used to reading a knitting chart and holding two colors at once, it is actually much simpler than you may have first thought. One of the striking features of Fair Isle knitting is the subtle shading of the many colors within each piece, even though no more than two colors are ever used in any one round. This is achieved by changing the background color as well as the contrast color on different rounds.

Size

To fit a child age 3–4 (5–6, 7–8, 9–10)
Chest 25½ (28¼, 30¼, 31¾) in/
65 (72, 77, 81) cm
Length 15 (16½, 19, 20½) in/
38 (42, 48, 52) cm
Sleeve seam 10½ (12, 13¾, 15¼) in/
27 (31, 35, 39) cm

Materials

4 (5, 6, 7) x 1¼oz (50g) balls
mushroom DK yarn
1 x 1¼oz (50g) ball mid-brown DK yarn
1 x 1¼oz (50g) ball fawn DK yarn
1 x 1¼oz (50g) ball mid-blue DK yarn
1 x 1¼oz (50g) ball navy-blue DK yarn
1 x 1¼oz (50g) ball olive-green DK yarn
1 x 1¼oz (50g) ball purple DK yarn
1 x 1¼oz (50g) ball plum DK yarn
Size 3 (3.25mm) needles
Size 6 (4mm) needles
Tapestry needle
Stitch holders

Gauge

24 sts and 30 rows = 4in (10cm) on
larger needles over st st

BACK

Using mushroom, cast on 80 (83, 85, 91) sts on smaller needles. Work in k1, p1 ribbing for 1½in (4cm). Inc 1 (2, 6, 4) sts evenly across the row to 81 (85, 91, 95) sts.
Change to larger needles and st st until work measures 9 (9¾, 11, 12¾) in/23 (25, 28, 32) cm.
Armhole shaping: Bind off 4 (4, 4, 5) sts at beginning of next 2 rows.
Raglan shaping: Dec 1 st (3 sts in from edge) at armhole edge of every 3rd row 8 (4, 4, 6) times, then every alt row until 35 (37, 39, 41) sts remain for back of neck.
Place sts on holder.

FRONT

Work as back until piece is 2in (5cm) short of armholes.
Place band of Fair Isle patterning following one of the traditional Fair Isle charts so that the center of the O or X lies on the center stitch of the front. In the example shown, the flower border pattern on page 124 was used. When work measures same as back to armholes, continuing to follow chart, shape armholes as for back.
When 55 (57, 57, 63) sts remain, end after a right side row.
Neck shaping: Work 19 (19, 19, 22) sts leave 17 (19,19, 19) sts on holder, work 19 (19, 19, 22) sts.
Dec 1 at neck edge of every row 8 times.
Continue armhole decreases until 3 sts are left. Bind off.
Return to first set of sts and shape as for 1st side reversing shaping.

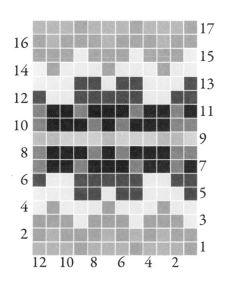

Purple
Olive
Mid-brown
Navy Blue
Plum
Fawn
Mid-blue
Mushroom

RIGHT: *This pattern is a compacted version of the OXO motif. The designs can be made larger through geometric progression, gradually making minor changes placed symmetrically to create a variation on the theme. Add an extra stitch of plum at stitches 3 and 11 on rows 5 and 13, and you will be able to see the cross beginning to take shape.*

ALTERNATIVE STITCHES

If you would like to use a different pattern to the one shown, the OXO, purse and cap patterns on pages 122 and 123 would work just as well. Depending on the size that you are working on, use graph paper to mark the central stitch and then chart the design out towards the sides, remembering to allow for the armhole shaping.

SLEEVES

Using mushroom, cast on 37 (37, 43, 43) sts on smaller needles. Work in k1, p1 ribbing for 1½in (4cm).
Sizes 3–4 (5–6): K5, m1 (k7, m1) x 4, k4 (42 sts).
Sizes 7–8 (9–10): K6, m1 (k8, m1) x 4, k5 (48sts).
Change to larger needles and st st.
Inc 1 st at each end of every 10th (10th, 12th, 12th) row to 48 (52, 56, 62) sts.
Work even until sleeve measures 10½ (11¾, 12¾, 13¼) in/27 (30, 32, 34) cm.
Shape cap: Cast off 4 (4, 4, 5) sts at beg of next two rows. Dec 1 st at each end of every 2nd (3rd, 2nd, 3rd) row 21 (6, 24, 6) times, then at each end of every 2nd row until 3 (6, 3, 4) sts remain. Leave on holder.

SHOULDER SEAMS

Sew in right sleeve and front seam of left sleeve.

NECKBAND

Using smaller needles and mushroom yarn, knit across 3 (6, 3, 4) sts of left sleeve, pick up and knit 16 (16, 18, 19) down left side of neck, knit across 17 (19, 19, 19) from holder, pick up and knit 16 (16, 18, 19) up right side of neck, knit 3 (6, 3, 4) from right sleeve and 35 (37, 39, 41) from back neck, 90 (100, 100, 106) sts.
Work 6 rows k1, p1 rib.

FINISHING

Sew remaining raglan seam. Sew side and sleeve seams. Weave in all ends.

Norwegian Mittens

Size

The mittens fit a medium-sized hand (approximately 8¼in/21cm around).

Materials

2 x 1¼oz (50g) balls cream DK yarn
1 x 1¼oz (50g) ball oxblood DK yarn
Set of size 5 (3.75mm) dpns
(Use size 3/3.25mm for a smaller size and size 6/4mm for a larger size mitten)
Tapestry needle
Stitch holders

Gauge

Tension: 26 sts and 26 rows – 4in (10cm)

ABOVE: *Traditionally many such designs would be worked in black and white.*

ALTERNATIVE STITCHES

The chart for the pattern on the mitten has been left blank deliberately, so that you can add a design of your own within the space. The diamonds and hearts pattern on page 124 and snowflake pattern on page 125 would both fit, and complement the pattern on the thumb and at the top of the mitten.

Beautifully patterned Norwegian mitten designs are hundreds of years old. They were always worked in two colors for the main motif, but sometimes had a touch of extra color on the cuffs. The designs are usually of snowflakes or Selbu stars, as they have come to be known, with a smaller version of the pattern—or a section of it—repeated at the top of the mitten and on the thumb. The palm would be worked in a simple pattern of alternate or diamond cross stitches.

RIGHT MITTEN

Using cream, cast on 44 sts and join into a round, being careful not to twist sts.
Place marker for beg of round.
Work 7 rounds k2, p2 rib.
Change to oxblood and work 3 more rounds, then 2 rounds cream, 1 round oxblood, 2 rounds cream, 3 rounds oxblood and 5 rounds cream.
Continue in cream and st st following chart.
Round 1: K44.
Round 2: Inc for thumb gusset as on chart (46 sts).
Cont to inc as on chart until there are 54 sts.
Choose a star, or similar pattern that uses 27sts and place this in the empty space on the mitten chart.
Round 9: K28 in chart pattern, place 11 on

holder, cast on 11, work to end.
Continue following chart, working shaping as shown, until there are 10 sts left.
Break off yarn, thread through sts, draw up, and fasten off.

THUMB

Place 11 sts from holder on needle, pick up 1 st from next round, pick up 11 sts from cast-on edge, pick up 1 st from next round (24 sts).
Work from chart decreasing to 8 sts.
Thread yarn through, draw up, and fasten off.

Work left mitten to match reversing position of thumb by placing it at end of round.
Weave in all ends.

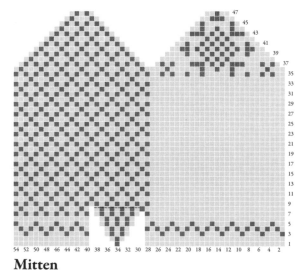

Mitten

Thumb

Knitting Techniques

All of the knitting stitches presented in this book can be achieved using a handful of basic knitting techniques, each of which is demonstrated over the following pages using step-by-step instructions. The methods shown are for right-handed knitters and simply need to be reversed if you are left-handed. In order to get a clearer idea as to how this might work, simply place a small mirror next to each picture. This will show the position of the hands in reverse.

Holding the Yarn

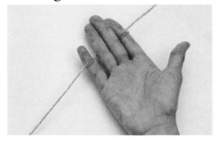

Whether you hold your yarn in the left or the right hand, one way to keep an even tension is to wrap the yarn around the little finger, then up over the next two fingers and around the index finger, near the tip. The closer the yarn is to the tip of your finger, the faster your speed will be.

Holding the Needles

Hold the right needle as you would hold a pencil, with the shaft of the needle resting in the "V" of thumb and index finger.

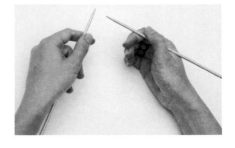

The left needle is then held in the palm of the hand with the thumb lightly resting on the top and the left index finger steadying it. The left thumb is used to push the stitches off the needle as you knit.

Casting On

TWO NEEDLES: KNITTED METHOD

1. Make a slip knot and put it on the left needle. * Insert the right needle into front of the slip knot and behind the left needle.

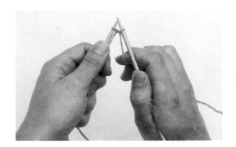

2. Wrap the yarn around the right needle, from the back to the front, and pull the loop through the slip knot.

3. Place this new loop on the left needle and repeat from * to the end.

TWO NEEDLES: CABLE METHOD

1. Cast on as for the simple method. Make two stitches on the left needle. * Insert the right needle between the stitches.

2. Wrap the yarn around right needle, from the back to the front, and pull the loop through.

3. Place this new loop on the left needle and repeat from * to the end.

CASTING ON: LONG TAIL METHOD

1. Leaving a long tail of yarn (approx. ½in/1cm for each stitch) put a slip knot on the needle. Wrap the ball end of yarn around the left index finger and the long tail around the thumb. Hold the ends firmly in your palm. * Pull on the needle so that a "V" shape is made between the thumb and forefinger.

2. Now take the needle over the lower strand of yarn and under the strand of yarn coming from behind the thumb.

3. Take the needle over the strand that is coming from the left side of the index finger and catch it with the tip of the needle.

4. Pull it towards you and back down through the loop around the thumb.

5. Drop the original loop off the thumb and catch another one from the long tail. Repeat from * to the end.

Binding Off

PLAIN BIND-OFF

1. This method can be used for a knit bind-off, a purl bind-off, a ribbing bind-off and a patterned bind-off, working the stitches as they appear. Start by knitting the first two stitches. Insert the left needle into the first stitch made and pull it over the second stitch.

2. Keeping the second stitch on the right needle, knit another stitch.

3. Now pull the first stitch over this new one, and so on to the end of the row. Break off the yarn, leaving 3–4 in (7–10cm) and thread this end through the last stitch on the right needle. Weave it in later.
For a loose bind-off, * knit the first two stitches together, then return the stitch to the left needle. Repeat from * to the end.

THREE-NEEDLE BIND-OFF

This technique is usually used for joining shoulder seams.
1. Place the two pieces together with right sides facing and needles tips facing the same direction.

2. Using a third needle, knit through the first stitch on the front needle and the first stitch on the second needle.

3. Knit the next two stitches as one, and pass the first stitch you made over them, as in plain bind-off. Repeat to the end.

Making Stitches

KNIT: ENGLISH METHOD

1. Hold the needles and yarn as described on page 132. * With the yarn at the back of the work insert the right needle into the front of the first stitch on the left needle. Wrap the yarn around the right needle, from back to front.

2. Bring the tip of the right needle back towards you and rest the tip on the left needle, without losing the loop that you have just made.

3. Use the tip of the right needle to slide the first stitch off the left-hand needle. Repeat from * to the end.

PURL: ENGLISH METHOD

1. Hold the needles and yarn as for the knit stitch but * keep the yarn at the front of the work. Insert the right needle from the back to the front of the first stitch.

2. Take the yarn over the needle from front to back, move the needle to the right and through the stitch.

3. Take the original stitch off the left needle. Repeat from * to the end.

KNIT: CONTINENTAL METHOD

1. Hold the needle containing the cast-on stitches and the yarn in the left hand. Holding the empty needle in the right hand, insert the right needle into the first stitch with the tip just behind the yarn.

2. Use the right needle to bring the yarn forwards and through the stitch, pushing the stitch on the left needle nearer the tip as you do so.

3. As you bring the right needle forwards, push the stitch off the left needle at the same time.

PURL: CONTINENTAL METHOD

1. Hold the needles and yarn as for the Continental knit stitch but * keep the yarn at the front of the work. Insert the right needle from the back to the front into the first stitch.

2. Take the yarn over the needle from front to back. Hold the yarn in place with the right thumb and draw it through the stitch. Take the original stitch off the needle. Repeat from * to the end.

KNITTING IN THE ROUND

To knit in the round, use a circular needle or a set of double-pointed needles. Cast on in the usual way using a circular needle. If using double-pointed needles, cast onto one of them, then divide the stitches over three needles. Do not turn the work, but knit into the slip knot, which is the first stitch that you cast on. Be careful not to twist the stitches around the needles. Mark this position with a stitch marker so that you know where the beginning of the round is. The same side of the work will always be facing you: to work stockinette stitch, you simply knit every row.

KNIT INTO BACK, OR KNIT THROUGH BACK LOOP

This stitch is sometimes used to make a decreased slope in a particular direction. It can also be used to make a stitch stand out from the background.

1. Instead of inserting the right needle through the front of a stitch on the left needle (as for knit), insert it into the back of the stitch.

2. Continue to make the stitch as for knit, wrapping the yarn around the needle from the back to the front.

PURL INTO BACK, OR PURL THROUGH BACK LOOP

1. In a slightly more awkward movement, take the right needle behind the left needle, in order to work from the back to the front of the stitch.

SLIP STITCH

Slip stitch has various applications. It can be used for decreasing, or to carry a contrast color into another row, or to form a textured pattern. Insert the right needle as for purl, but slide the stitch from the left to the right needle without taking the yarn around it.

When decreasing, slip the stitch as if it were to be a knit stitch.

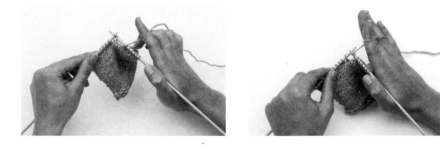

YARN OVER

Yarn overs are used in lace patterns, to compensate for a decrease worked along the row. They are usually worked on the right side before a knit stitch.

1. Before making a knit stitch, bring the yarn forwards under the right needle as if to purl, then take it back over the top of the needle before knitting the next stitch.

2. Some patterns feature a yarn over before making a purl stitch. Take the yarn over the needle away from you and then bring it back under the needle to the front.

3. Once you have brought the yarn to the front or around the needle, you can work the next stitch in the usual way.

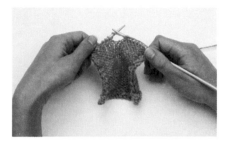

**YARN OVER TWICE,
OR DOUBLE YARN OVER**

1. Bring the yarn from the back to the front of the work, then around the needle again, so forming two new strands on the right needle.

2. On the return row, work knit 1, purl 1 into these two strands.

3. Or purl 1, knit 1, depending on the position of the stitches in the pattern.

KNIT INTO STITCH BELOW

Some of the raised stitches in this book require that you knit into a stitch on a different row in order to form a raised stitch on the right side.
1. Insert the right needle from front to back into the stitch one or a number of rows below the one on the left needle.

2. Knit the stitch in the normal way, but pull up a loop that is the height of the number of rows above it.

3. Put the new stitch on the left needle and knit it together with following stitch.

Decreasing

KNIT 2 TOGETHER

1. Insert the right needle into the second and then the first stitch on the left needle.

2. Knit them both off together.
To knit 2 together through the back loop, repeat these steps, but insert the right needle through the first and then the second stitch before knitting them.

PURL 2 TOGETHER

1. Insert the right needle through the first then the second stitch.

2. Purl them together.

PURL 2 TOGETHER THROUGH BACK LOOP

Either work 2 stitches together as for purl into back (see page 136), or
1. Purl the first stitch, slip it back onto the left needle, and bring the next stitch over it.

2. Slip the stitch back onto the right needle.

3. The two methods have a slightly different appearance. In the swatch above, the first method is shown below the fifth row and the second below the ninth.

SLIP, SLIP, KNIT

1. Insert the right needle knitwise into the first stitch, then do the same into the second stitch.

2. Insert the left needle into the front of these two stitches and knit them together.

3. This slopes the stitch to the left.

DOUBLE DECREASE

There are several methods of decreasing two stitches depending on the pattern. Purl decreases are made in a similar way.
1. The simplest method is to knit three stitches together as for "knit 2 together." This slopes the stitches to the right.

2. To slope the stitches to the left, slip 1, k2tog, and pass the slipped stitch over the knitted together stitch.

3. Slip, slip, knit, psso: slip the first two stitches separately, knit them together, put the resulting stitch back on the left needle, and bring the next stitch over them. Return the stitch to the right needle. This slopes the stitches to the right.

Increasing

WORK TWICE INTO STITCH

1. Knit the stitch but, without taking it off the left needle.

2. Now, either purl it or knit into the back of it.

3. You will now have increased one stitch, which will have a small hole beneath it when worked on the next row.

MAKE ONE

1. Insert the right needle under the strand that lies between the two needles.

2. Work the stitch in the usual way.

3. This leaves a small hole that is less noticeable if the stitch is knitted or purled through the back.

INVISIBLE INCREASE

1. Insert the right needle into the stitch just below the next stitch.

2. Now knit the stitch in the usual way.

3. This can be worked into the left or right leg of the stitch.

Stranding

1. When working in two colors, carry the yarn that is not in use across the back of the work. Here, you can see the reverse side of a Fair Isle swatch with short strands, or floats, of yarn between each change of color.

2. If the yarn is to be carried across more than 5 stitches it should be caught up every 3 or 4 stitches. Lift the non-working yarn onto the left needle. Bring the working yarn across the back of it and knit the next stitch, being careful not to catch the non-working yarn at the same time.

3. Let the non-working yarn fall back over the working yarn, then carry it along until it is needed again.

Picking up Stitches

1. Using a needle one or two sizes smaller than the ones you are knitting with, pick up the stitches with the right side of the work facing. Don't pick up the stitches from the extreme edge, but insert the needle at least one whole stitch away.

2. Wrap the yarn around the needle from the back to the front.

3. Knit the stitch in the normal way.

Grafting

1. With the same number of stitches on each of the needles, place the two pieces together with wrong sides facing. Leave a length of yarn at the end of the work. Thread the yarn length into a blunt-ended large-eyed sewing needle. * Insert the needle into the front of the first stitch of the front needle, as though to knit it.

2. Slip the stitch off the knitting needle and pull the yarn through to the same tension as the knitted stitches. Insert the sewing needle into the next stitch on the same knitting needle as if to purl it.

3. Pull the yarn through and insert the sewing needle into the front of the first stitch on the back needle as if to purl it. Draw the yarn through and slip it from the needle.

4. Insert the sewing needle into the next stitch on the same needle as though to knit it, pull the yarn through but don't slip it from the needle.

5. Repeat from * to the end.

Sewing Up

MATTRESS STITCH

1. Join matching yarn to the bottom edge of the pieces to be joined and with right sides facing out and lying side by side. Take the needle under the first two horizontal strands on the right hand piece.

2. Now take the yarn across and under the first two strands on the left hand piece.

3. Continue working from side to side, pulling the edges closed as you work.

Abbreviations

*	repeat from here	M1	make 1			together
( )	work stitches in parenthesis, repeating	p	purl	sssk	slip, slip, slip, knit slipped stitches
	instructions as many times as directed	p2tog	purl 2 sts together			together
cn	center needle	p3tog	purl 3 sts together	ssp	slip, slip, purl slipped stitches
dec	decrease	pfb	purl front and back			together
inc	increase	psso	pass the slipped stitch over	sssp	slip, slip, slip, purl slipped stitches
k	knit	p tbl	purl through back loop			together
k2tog	knit 2 sts together	p-wise	purlwise	st(s)	stitch(es)
k3tog	knit 3 sts together	rep	repeat	tbl	through back loop
kfb	knit front and back	RC	right cross	WS	wrong side
k tbl	knit through back loop	RH	right hand	wyib	with yarn in back
k-wise	knitwise	rn	right needle	wyif	with yarn in front
LC	left cross	RPC	right purl cross	yf	yarn forward
LH	left hand	RS	right side	yo	yarn over
ln	left needle	sl 1	slip 1	yo2	yarn over twice
LPC	left purl cross	ssk	slip, slip, knit slipped stitches	yrn	yarn round needle

Key

⑩	bobble
⊢−⊣	cluster 2 sts
⊢−−⊣	cluster 3 sts
⊢−−−⊣	cluster 4 sts
⁄4	cross 4
⁄⁄	cross 8
⍥	hook st in middle
ⱴ	inc to 5
▦	RS: k, WS: p
⊤	k1 elongated
ⱴ	k1, p1, k1 (in one stitch)
⁄	RS: k2tog, WS: p2tog
⋏	k3tog
⋊	k3togtbl
Ω	ktbl
℧	m1
⅄	m1 left leaning
Ⲕ	m1 purlwise left leaning
Ⲟ	m1 purlwise right leaning
Ⲅ	m1 right leaning
✕	no stitch
•	RS: p, WS: k
⁄	RS: p2tog, WS: k2tog
⋉	RS: p3tog, WS: k3tog
◆	p15 together
Ω	ptbl
☐	repeat section
⋏	sk2p2
V	RS: slip, WS: kfb
Ⅴ	RS: slip purlwise wyif, WS: slip purlwise wyib
⋋	sl1k1psso
⋀	sl1, k2tog, psso
⋀	sl2, k1, p2sso
▬	sl3 wyif
⋔	sl3 k1sl purlwise wyif
⌀	slip cross

3̄	solid line
⟍	ss
⟍	ssk
○	yo
∞	yo2
⟩⟨	1/1 RC: k into front of 2nd st, k into back of 1st st and sl both off together
⟩⟨	1/1 LC: k into back of 2nd st, k into front of 1st st and sl both off together
⟍⟋	1/3 RC: sl next 2 sts onto cn and hold at back, k1, k2 from cn
⟍⟋	1/3 LC: sl next st onto cn and hold at front, k2, k1 from cn
⟍⟋	3/3 RC: sl next 3 sts onto cn and hold at back, k3, k3 from cn
⟍⟋	3/3 LC: sl next 3 sts onto cn and hold at front, k3, k3 from cn
⟍⟋	4/4 RC: sl next 4 sts onto cn and hold at back, k4, k4 from cn
⟍⟋	4/4 LC: sl next 4 sts onto cn and hold at front, k4, k4 from cn
⟍⟋	6/6 RC: sl next 6 sts onto cn and hold at back, k6, k6 from cn
⟍⟋	6/6 LC: sl next 6 sts onto cn and hold at front, k6, k6 from cn
⟩⟨	2/2/2 RC: sl next 2 sts onto cn1 and hold at back, sl next 2 onto cn2 and hold at back, k2, k2 from cn2, k2 from cn 1
⟩⟨	2/2/2 LC: sl next 2 sts onto cn1 and hold at front, sl next 2 onto cn2 and hold at back, k2, k2 from cn2, k2 from cn1
⁄⟨	1/1 RPC: k into back of 2nd st, k into front of 1st st and sl both off together
⟩⟍	1/1 LPC: p into back of 2nd st, k into front of 1st st and sl both off together
⁄⟋	1/2 RPC: sl next 2 sts onto cn and hold at back, knit next st, p2 from cn
⟍	1/2 LPC: sl next st onto cn, p next 2 sts, k st from cn
⁄⟨	2/1 RPC: sl next 2 sts onto cn and hold at front, p1, k2 from cn
⟍	2/1 LPC: sl next st onto cn and hold at back, k2, p1 from cn
⟍⁄	1/3 RPC: sl next 3 sts to cable needle and place at back of work, k1, then p3 from cable needle
⟋⟍	1/3 LPC: sl next st to cable needle and place at front of work, p3, then k1 from cable needle

Index

Page numbers in boldface indicate photos on those pages.

Index cont.

Acknowledgments

Many thanks to the following people for contributing to this book:

For supplying the yarn:
Sue Blacker
The Natural Fibre Company
Unit B Pipers Court
Pennygillam Way
Launceston
Cornwall
PL15 7PJ

For buttons:
Duttons for Buttons
Oxford Street
Harrogate
North Yorkshire
HG1 1QE

For help with the knitting:
Hilary Grundy, Paulette Burgess, Helen Lee, Mhairi Sinclair, Daiga Kraukle, Lauren Watkins, Joyce Coombs, Maureen Newland, and Tarina Barnett
For help with the charts:
Madeline Weston

For designing and knitting the sock patterns on pages 31 and 49:
Tama Vaughn
twistedharefiberarts.etsy.com
www.ravelry.com (The Twisted Hare)

Picture Credits:
Alamy: p65, p67(r), p91, p113(r)
Corbis Images: p8(t), p48, p64, p67(l), p112
Hulton Archive: p6, p113(l)
Mary Evans Library: p66, p88, p89
Norfolk Museums & Archaeology Service: p13(t)
Shetland Museum: p115
Shutterstock: Elzbieta Sekowska, p8(b); ChipPix, p30
Tama Vaughn: p31, p49
V&A Museum: p7, p9, p12, p13(b), p90